P.S. Never Give Up Hope:

Advice from Youthful Offenders to Young America

Renata A. Hannans

Copyright © 2013 by Renata A. Hannans

iWrite4orU Publishing
PO Box 551006
Jacksonville, FL 32255
(904) 566-2964
iwrite4oru@gmail.com
www.iwrite4oru.com

ISBN: 978-0-615-74976-1

Cover Creation: Tyler Beall
Cover Designed for Print by Omar Scruggs
Photos Courtesy of the Department of Corrections

Author Contact Information:
Rhannans1@gmail.com
www.psnevergiveuphope.com

Disclaimer: The Author does not encourage you to contact any of the subjects in the book.

Personal Reviews

*P.S. **Never Give Up Hope** allows the curious reader to take a peek inside the confidential diaries of 10 youthful offenders through the eyes of its brilliant author who has captured and penned the one reckless moment in time where everything went wrong. That moment for these young men and women occurred early, during the formative teenage years, and thrust babies into dungeons where any hope of future freedom is as distant as the heavens are from the earth. The pages come alive and paint an ugly collage of violence, victims, grieving families and fractured hopes. It is a poignant reminder that we have failed our children who were at the stage of being too immature to fathom the ramifications of their crimes. How long will we lend a deaf ear to their cries as they struggle for survival in dangerous adult prisons? How can they ever heal? This book poses the ultimate challenge to its astute readership to demand resourceful Justice for Juvenile Offenders.*

—Judy Thompson, Forgotten Majority

The sharing of these heart-gripping stories may save thousands of young lives. This writing will certainly compel its readers to make better decisions and understand the unsympathetic consequences of their actions.

—Rhonda Peoples-Waters, P.A.

Gives shocking insight to the human element of juvenile incarceration.

—Attorney George Fallis

An eye opening account at the true effect that long harsh sentences have on our youth and their families.

—Attorney Kevin Cobbin

This brings home to the courts the impact which our sentences have on young offenders and the potential for rehabilitation.

—The Honorable Judge Charles Cofer

In our society there are many social distractions that cause our young people to lose focus of their unique purpose in life. They are so lost that they never assess their greater awareness to respect or value human mankind and develop themselves as productive citizens. This book serves as the only weapon left to those individuals who are serving their time in the criminal system. They serve as those reflective voices... crying from the wasteland, distributing light on their greatest gift that exists; youth. Harken O young people to the message that will enrich your lives.

—Cecil R. Mainor, Assistant Principal
Tallwood High School Virginia Beach, VA

The accounts in this book are true, and they are frighteningly real. I saw many of these stories in my work at a State penitentiary, and this book accurately describes the horrors and disappointments that so many young people live as a result of the horrid choices that they made in the wake of their youth. When they should have been shooting pool, they were shooting their next victim; when they should have been stealing second base, they were stealing their second car; when they should have been running their next touchdown, they were running from the police; when they should have been breaking the school record for academic achievement, they were breaking and entering. But amidst this reality, the author inculcates hope in a meaningful way. This is a great read.

—Jon Heymann, CEO
Communities In Schools (Jacksonville, FL)

A must read for teenagers and their parents.

—Attorney Gonzalo Andux

Table of Contents

Acknowledgements
Foreword: Patrick McGuinness
Note from Editor
Prologue
Youthful Offender Summaries
Introduction

Epilogue

Acknowledgements

I would first like to Thank God because without Him I am nothing and with Him I am everything. To my husband Leonard and my daughter Timaya: Thank you for sharing me with the world and being patient with me as I manifested my passion for others in this book. To Orain Benjamin Reddick: That talk you gave me from your hospital bed was the push I needed to start, and I appreciate it more than you know. To the postal crew at the General Mail Facility: I thank you for ensuring that the hundreds of letters I have mailed made it to their destinations.

To my grandmother Rebecca: You are my everything. A million thanks are not enough for raising me into the woman I have become, and you are constantly pushing me to be better. To my granddaddy David: Thank you for being a father to me. To Auntie Paula: I appreciate all that you have done for me, and for taking care of my most prized possession while I worked towards finishing this project. To my little sisters: Jade and Malia, I appreciate every time you went to check the mail and ensured that I received every letter over the past two years.

To my family, friends, co-workers and Communities In Schools of Jacksonville: Thank you for your words of encouragement and most importantly for inspiring me through the work that you do with the students of Duval County Public Schools.

To Liltera R. Williams of *iWrite4orU*: Thank you for every phone call, text message, email and home visit. Thank you for helping me LIVE MY DREAM!

To David, Devonta, Jonathan, Richard, Samantha, Shimeek, Sophia, Tyler and Thornton: Thank you all for giving the gift of yourself to Young America. It is my consistent prayer that your stories will help others. I carry each of you with me every single day.

To the students of Forrest High School and William M. Raines High School: Thank you for inspiring me to reach beyond the walls of the school to inspire others. To the law firm of Finnell, McGuinness, Nezami & Andux: Thank you for your guidance, mentoring and believing in me.

To the young people headed down the wrong path, here is the warning before destruction: Take what each subject is telling you and make wise decisions. Remember for every choice we make there are consequences. To the parents: Be sure to lead by example, nurture and love your children and pay attention to the signs. To every young boy or girl sitting in a bunk or cell:

When you feel you have nothing left...

P.S. Never Give Up Hope

Foreword by Patrick McGuinness

For over 35 years I have labored at the law, specifically criminal law, and most often in connection with violent crimes. I have been lead or second chair Counsel on behalf of more than 400 individuals charged with murder and countless others facing extraordinarily serious charges. During those three and one half decades, I have watched with some horror and immense frustration what is inaccurately called the Juvenile Justice System. There is very little justice in the system and fewer and fewer juveniles that remain in that system. Children are routinely charged and punished as adults. There has been a powerful and unrelenting shift away from the notion of rehabilitation towards increasingly punitive and harsher penalties for young offenders. There are a variety of theories regarding the underlying reasons for the more draconian punishments now being meted out to young offenders—in some cases, children. Whether the impetus for that movement is political, racial, financial or some combination of factors is the subject of speculation and debate.

Renata Hannans' book focuses not on the reasons impelling courts and legislatures to fashion sentences of extraordinary severity for young offenders, but rather her book provides a unique insight into the human cost of these punitive policies. Ms. Hannans is a young African-American woman that I first met approximately three years ago.

She has worked with me on a volunteer basis in my law practice and has in her capacity, as a high school Case Manager, consistently demonstrated a desire to understand, change and improve the lives of the young people she works with every single day. In this book she gives a voice to the mute youngsters we see on the evening news in their orange jail jump suits as they are sentenced to penalties that are difficult to even comprehend. This book should be read by every parent that lives in absolute fear of that possibility that their child, whom they love so much, might take a misstep or have a catastrophic lapse of judgment—such as the young men and women she chronicles in this book. Ms. Hannans is not some naïve apologist for young offenders whose stories she tells. This book should also be required reading for the many young men and women attempting to navigate their juvenile years. The courts have recently recognized the body of scientific literature establishing the distinct characteristics of the adolescent brain. The way information is processed, the degree of impulsivity and the relative inability to truly appreciate the consequences of choices are unique features of the adolescent brain. Several of the young offenders portrayed in the book have come to wisdom too late for themselves, their families or the families of those they have injured. However, their stories and observations might serve others well. Youth, poverty, greed, drugs and fragmented families are common themes in the stories they tell. One young man remarks upon his mother's daily admonition to him to "make good choices."

He did not, and his failure to make good choices had tragic consequences for him, his family and others. Ms. Hannans details some of those consequences—the despair, anger and violence of prison life, particularly for youthful offenders. One of Ms. Hannans' correspondents puts it well, "Prison ain't a place for a human being, not even an animal." It is existence "in a cage." Perhaps if more young men and women wrestling with the temptations of the "streets" could read the words and accounts of those that Ms. Hannans has spoken with, they could avoid the cages. The United States Constitution has a prohibition against cruel and unusual punishment; however, as this book makes clear with regard to juvenile offenders, cruel punishment is no longer unusual. We now live in a society that apparently regards juvenile offenders as disposable; second chances or rehabilitation are not even contemplated. There needs to be changes in the system, and by putting faces on these young offenders and letting their voices be heard, by letting the reader glimpse their humanity, emotions, dreams and regrets, maybe those changes will come. Maybe some young people will avoid this sad fate. As the author notes:

P. S. Never Give Up Hope...

Note from Editor

In the Summer of 2012, Author Renata A. Hannans contacted me to request my *iWrite4orU* services for her nonfiction book, *P.S. Never Give Up Hope*. We scheduled a meeting at the Riverside Starbucks in July. It was pouring rain and I asked Ms. Hannans if she wanted to reschedule our meeting. Her answer was an immediate "No." I arrived before she did, and when we were finally introduced, I sensed a bit of urgency in her demeanor. She admitted to being nervous about sharing her idea with a stranger and told me that she was afraid of writing a book that would not meet her overall expectations. I assured her that I would do all that I could to assist her along the way. I gladly offered my services to Ms. Hannans, knowing that she was skeptical about her writing abilities, as well as how confident I was in my own ability to successfully assist her with the task at hand. She was passionate about the topic, but it was left up to me to help her realize that writing is indeed an acquired skill. Although she had been collecting data for over a year, Ms. Hannans worked faithfully and diligently on her project for six more consecutive months. During the course of our partnership, she continued to correspond with each youthful offender while simultaneously drafting their chapters and adhering to my editing suggestions, along with handling her full-time responsibilities as a wife, a mother, and Case Manager. She was fully immersed in her #WriterGrind, but the reality of her initial skepticism began to sink in after receiving numerous rejections from a few major publishing companies. Ms. Hannans was afraid that no one would be receptive of her message and wanted to give up.

However, I used her title as metaphoric way of motivating her to continue: *P.S. Never Give Up Hope... You are going to save so many lives.*

Ms. Hannans later made the decision to self-publish, because she wanted to maintain control over her own destiny. Furthermore, Ms. Hannans was unaware of how much she had already changed my life. By having faith in me as a first-time Author and newly established Editor, she equipped me with the confidence I needed to catapult my Live YOUR Dream movement, and I was totally dedicated to helping her dream come true. Ms. Hannans introduced me to the reality of juvenile sentencing, and I was shocked by every revelation as we pursued our quest. I traveled with her to interview two of the subjects in the book, Devonta Mayberry (Chapter 8) and Sophia Smith (Chapter 9). Sophia was enjoying the freedom of walking around in her own home, but Devonta was still incarcerated.

On November 26, 2012, Ms. Hannans and I drove 2 hours to Mayo, FL to interview him in a glassed room. After being checked by security, we were led through the gates, passing inmates who were participating in recreational activities, and obviously excited about seeing two new faces. We waited for Devonta for about 20 minutes. He greeted us like a gentleman and answered our questions respectfully and truthfully. I was admittedly nervous, but Ms. Hannans was comfortable and already familiar with the procedure. When she shared the details of her experiences with every other subject in the book, I was very impressed with her willingness to conduct research and obtain information firsthand.

Responding to letters on a daily basis, sending thoughtful gifts, traveling solo to Vero Beach, FL on a whim, and sticking to her commitment of greeting one of the youthful offenders on the day she was released from prison are just a few examples of how devoted she was to this project.

Ms. Hannans has sacrificed a lot to accomplish this goal, most noticeably quality time with her own daughter, and even at a young age she understands what Mommy is trying to do. By dedicating herself to these individuals who literally don't have much to look forward to, Ms. Hannans has exemplified a strong desire to inspire change. She constantly encourages everyone around her to do whatever it takes to "make it happen", myself included. I am proud of what she has allowed me to help her achieve, honored to present the final product, and confident that this book will affect the lives of many.

P.S. Never Give Up Hope...
and Live YOUR Dream!

Liltera R. Williams, *iWrite4orU*
Writer/Editor/Publisher

Prologue

While working as a Case Manager with high school teenagers in Duval County, I came to the realization that a proportionate number of young men and women were being incarcerated. If they hadn't already been to jail they were well on their way, or knew someone who was. There isn't a week that passes that we don't hear the news of someone being robbed, shot, or even killed by a juvenile. In this profession I am tasked with helping children succeed by ensuring that they are on track to being promoted and ultimately able to graduate from high school. The students on my caseload look to me for advice, guidance, or may simply need someone to listen to them. I give them heartfelt advice; however, advice about breaking the incarceration cycle amongst our youth is more effectively delivered from those who are actually incarcerated. I began this quest over a year ago by writing 17 year old Jonathan Hartley, who is currently serving a life sentence. I then began to write other inmates and asked them to share their stories.

I traveled across the state of Florida to meet and interview the majority of them. The letters began to pour in and with each letter came raw, uncut and candid information from those who have lived the so-called "street life". As a result, I decided to turn these letters into a book that will serve as a help guide for adolescents.

The ideology that "It takes a village to raise a child" is no longer present in today's society. This book is a reminder that you are not the only one going through adversity. It reminds us that the pressures of the world are real, but we must not let them distract us because they will only lead us to two places: the cemetery or prison.

Youthful Offender Summaries

Chapter 1: *Free Lil Eddie*
Jonathan E. Hartley

In December of 2009, Jonathan Hartley, along with two others, attempted to rob and subsequently killed Sarah Hotham, a Domino's pizza delivery driver. At the time, Jonathan was 15 years old. He was raised by a single mother and is currently serving a life sentence at age 18.

Chapter 2: *14 Doing 70*
Shimeek Gridine

At 14 years old, Shimeek and his 12 year old friend found a gun and decided to rob someone. The bullet grazed the side of the victim's face, but he survived. However, Shimeek was sentenced to 70 years in prison. His appeal is currently being reviewed by the Supreme Court. For now, he is scheduled to be released in the year 2079.

Chapter 3: *Close to Home*
Thornton Brunson

In the summer of 1990 at age 17, Thornton shot and killed Marcel Findlay at a neighborhood cookout. Five shots were fired and Marcel later died at a local hospital. Over two decades have passed and Thornton is now 39 years old serving 25 years to life.

Chapter 4: *Daddy Died, Momma Tried*
Tyler Beall

Currently, Tyler is 21 years old serving a six year sentence for robbery. Growing up, Tyler's mom was a routine alcoholic, and after his father passed away he fell deeper into the abyss of drug abuse and alcoholism. Tyler regrets it all and plans to make a change for the better when he is released from prison in 2016.

Chapter 5: *Never Use Drugs*
Samantha Sneed

Samantha's drug use began with a friend at age 12 with marijuana. As a juvenile, Samantha spent most of her teenage years in unsuccessful drug rehab programs. She was released from prison on September 29, 2012, after serving a two year sentence for burglary, and hopes she never has to return.

Chapter 6: *Speaking From Death Row*
Anonymous

The following anonymous inmate was handed a death sentence and is awaiting execution, unless he is granted an appeal. He decided not to share his life story; however, he offers candid advice to young America from Death row.

Chapter 7: *Product of My Environment*
Richard Hannans

At age 17, Richard was sentenced to 10 years in prison for armed robbery. When he was released in 2007, it was hard to find legitimate work with a felony record. In 2011, Richard was sentenced yet again to 15 years in prison as a habitual offender for selling drugs to an undercover officer. Upon release, he will be nearly 50 years old and will have served half his life behind bars.

Chapter 8: *My Brother's Keeper*
Devonta Mayberry

At age 17, while riding in the car with friends, Devonta had no idea it would be his last time seeing one of them alive. Even today it is still hard to grasp the idea that he is serving 40 years for the murder of his friend that he called his brother; a murder that he did not actually commit.

Chapter 9: *Guilty by Association*
Sophia Smith

At age 18, Sophia and her mother were busted for involvement in a drug ring. She didn't understand the severity of the trouble she was in as she awaited trial. When Sophia and her mother were sentenced to 30 years, she was eight months pregnant and later delivered her second baby girl in federal prison.

Chapter 10: *The Hustler, The Rapper, The Man*
David Goodman

David was an intelligent young man who was constantly battling the emptiness of living without a father and growing up in poverty. After establishing an independent record label as a local rapper, David was charged with his fourth strike. He is currently serving 15 years in federal prison for conspiracy, and working hard to maintain healthy relationships with his 13 children.

Introduction

As I turned on 17th Street SW, I noticed to my right a city dump and to my left was the Indian River Correctional Institution. Through these doors awaited the convicted murderer and attempted murderer with whom I had appointments. As I was being screened by security, my emotions were running high. I'd prepared several questions to ask them and had planned this visit for months. When I walked through the doors of the visitation park, there sat two of the most innocent looking children. Their voices weren't deep at all and even if they tried they could not look a day over 18. My entire train of thought was lost because they appeared as children, not inmates, faced with the rest of their lives in prison. Almost immediately the mother in me wanted to hug them, but I did not. I wanted to turn back the hands of time and erase their wrongs, but I could not. Jonathan and Shimeek were the first subjects of this book I was fortunate enough to meet.

Since that meeting, it has become very clear to me that their voices need to be heard, and their struggles deserve to be made public. The ride home was almost four hours in length and was a quiet one. I kept thinking *"What went wrong? What could have been done to prevent this? What can be done to make this better?"* In this book you will find out the answers to all of the questions I asked myself on August 24, 2011.

This book is for every young boy or girl headed down the road of destruction. It offers parents insight to how life has an effect on some of the behaviors children display. I want every young person to read this advice and think of the consequences associated with your actions. To those of you who are already incarcerated...

P.S. Never Give Up Hope

Chapter 1

#J41587

Jonathan E. Hartley

Free Lil Eddie

**"*Yeah I was pretty popular,
but that ain't doing nothing for me now.*"**

57 year old Sarah Hotham was delivering pizzas on December 4, 2009, just like any other work day, except this would be her last. She was responding to a delivery call to an abandoned apartment in Jacksonville, Florida, in a Murray Hill neighborhood when she met her fate. The last thing she saw was the barrel of a gun and on the other side of it was convicted killer, Jonathan Hartley, affectionately known as "Lil Eddie". Eddie and his friends decided to rob a pizza delivery driver of pizza and cash. The call to place the order was made from Yvonne Hartley's cell phone, Eddie's mother. That call was tracked hours later and led to his arrest. His co-defendant provided him with the gun prior to going home for curfew and they agreed that whatever money was taken would be shared amongst each other. This same gun was used in a successful robbery the previous day, which netted them some pizza and 14 dollars in cash. Once Ms. Hotham arrived, she was shot dead in the chest and no money was stolen. When Eddie got home, he immediately knew he had just made the biggest mistake of his life; a life that would soon be cut short at the tender of age of 15. He cried and couldn't sleep at all that night, so he prayed... for the victim, for protection, and for forgiveness. He then prayed that it would all go away, but he knew it wouldn't. Every time he heard sirens, he was nervous. Two days later, while walking to the store with his co-defendant, he was arrested. His co-defendant was carrying a firearm in his waistband, which is believed to be the gun that fired the fatal shot to Ms. Hotham.

Since that day, he has been incarcerated and will be for a term of natural life, unless he is granted an appeal. Eddie was sentenced to life in prison for the lesser charge of second degree murder, 15 years for attempted armed robbery, and 20 years for armed robbery, with all sentences to be served concurrently. All of these charges are punishable to life in prison. He decided to plead guilty, with hopes that his clean juvenile record would aid him in receiving a lesser sentence.

Upon pleading guilty, Eddie apologized to the victim's family and even the State Attorney, Angela Corey. Sam Garrison, the prosecutor in his case said, "I genuinely like this young man... and it absolutely breaks my heart to see him sitting there." Mr. Garrison requested a 50 year sentence. He also stated that Eddie needed to serve as an example for why senseless violence needs to stop. However, The Honorable Judge Charles Arnold didn't think 50 years was enough and moved forward with the life sentence. During sentencing, Judge Arnold said, "I don't know what it is, but there is a segment of our community generally between the ages of 14 and 25 that just wants to run around and be gangsters." Arnold also hoped that every high school in Duval County would post the *Times Union* report of the article. While working as a case manager at William M. Raines High School, I did just that. When the students would enter my office, they'd say "I know him" or "That's my dawg."

Some students wore shirts bearing his picture that read *Free Lil Eddie*, and even created a Facebook page in support of his release. They hoped he would get a second chance and oftentimes remarked that they couldn't believe he would do such a thing because he was a sweet person. Many of them knew him from their middle school years and the neighborhood they stemmed from. Their overwhelming reactions to the article inspired me to write him. It took a while to receive a response, and I later learned he had to put much thought into it:

Sorry it took so long had to do a lot of thinking...................

Mrs. Renata Hannans

About Prison

Prison as you already know is not a good place man it really aint a place for nobody in the world so I'm gone tell you a little bit about it. We live in small rooms with 1 roommate its two beds/bunk beds a toilet and two big lockers, so its literally no space to walk around in and also you have to sit in the same room and watch somebody use the bathroom but that's just the beginning. If you are less fortunate and your family and friends can't send you money then you eat the state food which is 3 meals a day and they real small and don't taste good its basically the same food we all eat at home with no seasoning and of course it aint McDonalds or nothing also you gotta wake up early and stay up all day from 4:45 a.m. to 5:00 p.m. that's when you get to sit on your bed after 5:00 p.m. and that's also when you get your last meal you also have to shave your face clean you can't wear the clothes you want and the clothes you wear somebody else wore before you also you got bull junk jobs like cleaning up all day, pickin up trash at a dump and stuff like that the school straight with trades and they try to get you a GED but that's the little bad things.

This is things that inmates do to each other, if you can't fight and you don't have heart don't come to prison because when you first come you gone get TOH (test of heart) basically stuff get real you gotta do a lot of fighting and you may get poked wit a homemade shank or hit in the head with a combination lock numerous times but you gotta make it through it cause if you don't you gone be a jizzle that's when you basically gave up, you couldn't handle it you got scared and punked up so now all the money that your people send you somebody else takes it and leaves you with nothing. They give away their food and stuff and get slapped around for no reason.

It's also very stressful in here you only get to see your family on weekends and being from Jacksonville it's a 3 hour drive so I only see mines once a month and that mail aint no joke boy. When you don't get mail you start to feel like nobody loves you and don't care for you and all type of stuff so that's a hint. I need a lot of support write me (Jonathan Hartley J41587).

27

Man this aint a place you wanna come you might think you hard man listen to your momma or madukes cus she gone be hurt the most! You gone be missin your family and friends and missin out on so much you got your chance now you free don't make a mistake like me and be gone for a longtime yall just chill out there. Use me as an example I know yall probably not listening but that's basically what's going on. I say this again don't come to prison please it's not the place to be trust me. Once again don't come to prison and thank you Mrs. Hannans for giving me the opportunity to help others I deeply appreciate it.

P.S.
Listen to every word I said it will help you in the long run.

Yours Truly

Jonathan E. Hartley

Many times I've heard that there is no love like a mother's love. This statement rang true to me when I met Jonathan's mother, Yvonne Hartley. As we spoke, the pain in her voice and the tears in her eyes inclined me to shed tears as well. Instantly, her hurt became my hurt and I could feel her emptiness. On December 6, 2009, Yvonne was driving down the street when she saw Keon Sams lying handcuffed on the ground. She called his father to tell him that he was being arrested. As she exited her car to check on Keon, she realized that Eddie was already handcuffed in the backseat of the police car. When she asked the officer why, he replied that they were needed for questioning.

Once Yvonne arrived to the Police Memorial Building, she noticed the door read *Homicide*. She thought, "Surely they must have the wrong person." While alone with Eddie in the interrogation room she asked him, "Is there anything you need to tell me?" Eddie's reply was, "No." That was the last time Yvonne saw her son outside the walls of a courthouse or prison. She never asked him why or forced him to share the details of what happened. From that moment on she has been by his side and often reminds him that she will never leave him.

As a child Eddie was very energetic, mannerable, and a class clown. He excelled academically until he reached high school and started to rebel. He played basketball in Chapel Hill, North Carolina, during summer breaks and football at Grand Park in Jacksonville, Florida, until age 14.

Eventually he stopped because they moved and his mother's work schedule did not allow him to attend practices. Both Eddie and his mother agree this could have aided in him having more time on his hands to find trouble. Every morning before leaving for school, Yvonne told Eddie to make good choices and that she loved him. Now that Eddie is in prison, Yvonne can only afford to travel to see him once a month. She and his little sister are his only two visitors. When they do see each other, they laugh, cry and think of when, not if, he will be able to come home. His friends don't visit or reply to letters because their parents won't allow it, which makes Eddie sad. Yvonne constantly reminds Eddie that his sentence is not in vain and that while incarcerated, God is using him to help others. Both she and Eddie want other young people to learn from his mistakes and not make similar mistakes of their own.

Chapter 2

#132747

Shimeek Gridine

14 Doing 70

**"When I first got to prison
it was like entering a backyard with vanquished pit bulls
trying to get at you and rip you apart."**

At age 14, most young boys are transitioning from middle school to high school. They are staying up late at night talking on the phone with girls, playing sports, video games and going to school every day. A sweet yet tender age, 14, is a couple years past the pre-teen phase and a few years shy of adulthood. At this point in our lives we are just beginning to understand who we are. It is the trial and error period when we make mistakes and learn from them. At 14, peer pressure and trying to fit it in has a great impact on teenagers. At 14, you can't smoke, drink, vote or even be gainfully employed. Think back to 14 when you made mistakes or got in trouble and remember the consequences. I recall a friend persuading me to smoke a black and mild cigar, and as I began to puff my mother pulled up. I threw it down and started choking and running at the same time. At 14, I was in the ninth grade at a new school; I had to make new friends and learn new things. I say all this to say that one mistake at this age can cause you to forfeit the right to have any type of freedom. When Shimeek was 14, he was awaiting his fate at the Pre-Trial Detention Facility where he resided and attended school for nearly a year.

On April 21, 2009, Shimeek and his 12 year old friend, "Duck-Duck", decided to rob someone. As a man walked out of his business, Shimeek and "Duck-Duck" approached him. The man attempted to get away, but he was shot and sustained minor injuries. He was released from the hospital the same night.

Throughout all court proceedings, he was never present, chose not to cooperate with the state, and refused to make any statements. It was Shimeek's 12 year old friend who told authorities what happened. The guilt weighed heavily on Shimeek and he confided in his grandmother about what happened. Shimeek wanted to do the right thing, so he turned himself in. His grandparents drove him to the police station where he told authorities what happened, and he was subsequently arrested. Shimeek was booked for first degree attempted murder, attempted armed robbery, and aggravated battery. He was certified and charged as an adult and held without bail for a year. Even though he told authorities it was Duck-Duck's plan to rob someone, he was portrayed as the mastermind because he was the oldest. Duck-Duck was placed in a program for juveniles and released shortly after Shimeek was sentenced. At the sentencing, his family came from as far as New York and the Carolinas. Rather than present his case to a jury of his peers, Shimeek decided to plead directly to the judge. Both he and his family hoped for a youthful offender sentence, which would have allowed him a second chance at life and redemption. Instead, Shimeek was sentenced to 70 years for first degree attempted murder and 25 years for attempted armed robbery. He was required to complete a minimum mandatory sentence of 25 years, with credit for the year he had already served. This means he must serve 25 years day for day before he can begin to accrue gain time for good behavior on the remaining 50 years.

The sentence handed down by the Honorable Judge Adrian Soud Jr. came as a shock to everyone because Shimeek did not have an extensive juvenile record, and no one was killed. Just three months prior to Shimeek being sentenced, the Supreme Court ruled in *Graham v. Florida* that life sentences for juveniles who commit non-homicidal crimes were unconstitutional. If Shimeek does in fact serve out his sentence he will be over 80 years old; that's if he lives out the life expectancy of nearly 67. His current sentence leaves no room for rehabilitation or for him to reenter society as a productive citizen.

Shimeek was born in Brooklyn, New York, in 1994 to his single mother, Charlett. His early life was hard, as his mother struggled to raise both him and his little brother. Between the ages of four and six, Shimeek lived in a shelter and attended school every day. Although they were homeless, Shimeek recalls his mother still made sure they were well fed. They could have picked up and moved with family, but his mother was then and still is very prideful and didn't want to be a burden on anyone. When Shimeek was around seven years old, his mother sent him to Jacksonville, Florida, to live with her parents for a chance at a better life. This was decided when on one occasion Charlett walked Shimeek to school and he made his way back home. This frightened her and she wanted him to live in a safe environment with a better school system. Before Shimeek left, he had finally begun to build a relationship with his father.

Once he moved to Jacksonville, his father was murdered. About a year after Shimeek came down south, his mother and brother followed. They all lived with his grandmother until his mother was able to find a place to stay and employment. Throughout his life, Shimeek had an older cousin named Michelle who spent a lot of quality time with him. She would make sure he had things he needed, as well as some of the things he wanted. Even when the family hadn't heard from her, Shimeek did. Prior to the robbery, Michelle passed away along with another family member. This all happened within a two week time span. Shimeek took her passing very hard and his behavior and attitude became progressively worse. He was suspended from school often for fighting and had a lot of anger built up inside of him. Instead of taking the straight path, he took the bumpy road and let his anger control him.

Growing up without a father was the reason behind some of his anger. Although he had his grandfather and uncle, he wanted his father. Additionally, when his father passed away, his half-brother was sent to foster care and he hasn't seen him since. The rest of his anger was a result of seeing his mother struggle financially. Also during this time, his mother was involved in an abusive relationship. While Shimeek never witnessed the actual fights, he saw the aftereffects and this angered him. Once Shimeek came home and his mother was badly bruised and battered, so he went looking for her boyfriend.

It was then that she decided to break off the relationship because it affected the attitudes of her children. While Shimeek was free, he never liked listening to the advice of others and even admits he was careless. He also says if he could take it all back he would:

Now that I'm up here I realize I should've never taken this route tryna be cool and sell drugs because you see other people doing it. Man this ain't cool. If I could I would go to school every day, I wouldn't skip any classes and I would have set a better example for my little brother instead of running the streets. I can't tell y'all what to do but I can tell y'all to slow down before you start doing your own thing. Finish school and do something positive with your life...

When he first got to the "River" (Indian River Correctional Institution), "It was like entering a backyard with vanquished pit bulls running free tryna get at you and rip you apart. Either you get down with a gang or become a jizzle." Shimeek describes a jizzle as "someone who don't do anything without being told, he don't eat, his money is taken, being hit in the head with locks inside of socks, stabbed, raped and nearly dead while the correctional officers just sit and watch. They don't care what happens because they still get paid." At the River, he saw it all. "Prison ain't a place for no human being, not even an animal," he continued.

Currently, Shimeek is being held in close management which means he is locked down 24 hours a day and only gets to call home once or twice a month. Rec lasts for two hours, in which the inmate is placed in a single cage where he can freely exercise and talk to the person in the cage next to him. In confinement, you are not allowed to talk or you will be placed on property restriction where you are locked in a cell for up to four days wearing nothing but your underwear. Inmates in confinement are allowed to shower on Tuesday, Thursday and Saturday between five and ten minutes. "I see people get gassed for no reason and go to psych every day. You just got to know how to maintain in C.M.," says Shimeek. His only form of communication is through letters. He spends most of his time studying for his G.E.D. and praying, because he says that's the first step of change.

The Supreme Court is currently reviewing the District Court's opinion in Shimeek's case. The only relief for juveniles serving lengthy sentences is to provide them with the opportunity for parole, which was abolished in 1984 in the state of Florida. It is the legislatures who have the power to reinstate parole, not the courts. With the current sentence of 70 years and a release year of 2079, Shimeek will spend the rest of his life in prison with no chance for redemption. "Life in prison without the possibility of parole gives no chance for fulfillment outside prison walls, no chance for reconciliation with society, no hope." (Excerpt from Graham v. Florida, 2010).

Chapter 3

#121312

Thornton Brunson

Close to Home

"There is no justification, no true excuse for taking a person's life. The shame of it will be with me for the rest of mine."

I was in kindergarten when my neighbor and close family friend, Marcel Findlay, was killed. I don't remember much, other than the fact that I wasn't allowed to attend the funeral and was told he'd never be at our house again. I have no detailed memories of Marcel besides the many photos of him at our house and remembering him hanging out with my uncle Gary. I've always been told that he went to a party and ran into a kid he fought in school earlier in the week; shots were fired and he was killed. For many years there was an awkward silence in our house about what happened that night. I guess the pain was too great to re-open that closed chapter. I was too young to understand, but even though Marcel was gone his family remained and is still three doors down. When I questioned my uncle recently about how he felt, he stated that God works in mysterious ways. He also had a brush with the law, and during his incarceration he was placed at the same facility as Thornton. When he recognized exactly who he was, he asked him why he did what he did. He recalls Thornton saying that he was trying to fit in with his older friends. However, few details were exchanged because the next morning my uncle Gary was transferred to another facility to serve out his sentence. When I began to write this book, I immediately thought to reach out to Marcel's accused killer, but I was afraid. Afraid of what the Findlays would think, afraid of Thornton's response, and simply afraid to face the man responsible for the tragic and premature death of my uncle's best friend and my neighbor.

I drafted a letter and I never mailed it due to the fears I just mentioned. Months later, I wrote another letter explaining exactly who I was and how I knew the victim of the crime he was serving a life sentence for. Once I mailed the letter, I patiently awaited a response, and after about a week I received one. My eagerness was apparent as I was opening our first correspondence because I didn't know what to expect. By the time I reached line five of the letter I sensed a tone of remorse and willingness to aid me in helping yet another young black male not repeat such a grave mistake. The letter started off with:

For obvious reasons it pains me to dwell on the past, but if my experience or words could help turn a person's life around, stop them from taking a life and destroying theirs like I did, then I'm all in...

As a child Thornton made friends easily and played both football and basketball at Yancy Park in Jacksonville, Florida. He never carried himself as a "bully" or "thug". Mostly all of his classmates grew up with him in the neighborhood and he was the one in class keeping everyone laughing while flirting with girls. The good times came to a halt when he started hustling, but every so often he and his friends would still play basketball. His parents divorced when he was 14, and it was at that time that Thornton began to feel resentment towards his father for leaving. With his father gone and his mother working long hours to support him and his brother, he lost a lot of supervision.

Thornton recalls around this time things began to change; not just with the divorce of his parents, but also in the neighborhood. He used to look up to the older guys who could play ball and had all the girls:

For a teenage boy this is big. When crack arrived to the hood all that changed. It was a total takeover. Suddenly everyone I knew had pocket money or more. I think every teenage boy wishes he had his own money to buy stuff, the shoes he likes, a car etc. without having to go and ask his mom who is struggling trying to pay bills. I was no different. I tried getting a job but didn't get it. From that point on I started hustling and lost my innocence. I can't say it was to help my mother pay bills or because of some desperation. It was purely greed and the want for material things. No one ever realizes how addictive and dangerous this lifestyle is until you're caught up in it. You're just as addicted as the junkies you selling to. My mother tried the best she could to keep me out the streets, but being a single mother with two kids and working all day is not an easy thing. My father couldn't tell me nothing because I felt that he walked out and I was going to prove I was a man without him. The guys I looked up to were getting locked up, killed or started using drugs themselves. You ignore all the bad signs around you, the warning, the danger because you get so caught up in chasing the dream of getting rich. The illusion of getting rich from this lifestyle blinded me when in truth I did have options. You always have choices.

The ability to make choices is both a gift from God and a responsibility to yourself because you have to live with the consequences of your choices.

Thornton was in the ninth grade when he told a friend he had 30 dollars, and his friend told him he knew of a way to double it. The thought of making money enticed Thornton, so he began selling drugs. In school at Jean Ribault Senior High, Thornton did just enough work to get by. He participated in the band, but was kicked out for flirting with girls and he was cut from the football team because he couldn't gain weight.

By the time he was in tenth grade he was completely in the streets. He began missing class in order to sell drugs, but he was home by the time his mom got off work so it went undetected. Eventually, Thornton had earned enough money to purchase a car, a Toyota Corolla for seven hundred and fifty dollars. He parked it at a friend's house for months and lied to his mom about who the car actually belonged to. In the middle of his transition to eleventh grade, Thornton and his mom moved in with his aunt. During this time, Thornton was busted by the cops after being set up by someone who was working for him selling drugs at a hotel. When he arrived to pick up his friend, the friend asked to drive, but Thornton didn't find it suspicious. He drove them to a Jiffy gas station where the police were waiting to arrest him. Thornton spent two weeks at the Juvenile Detention Center.

He could have come home after a week, but his mom made him stay a few extra days to teach him a lesson. The charges were later dropped. A few weeks after being home Thornton was back in the streets, but he decided to work alone to lessen his chances of getting caught. A cousin provided him with more drugs to get back on his feet. About six months later he was pulled over for driving with an expired paper tag. He tried to run, but he was caught and ended up spending 21 days in the detention center. Upon release, he was responsible for cleaning up on the weekends in Downtown Jacksonville and under bridges. He wasn't completing much school work and only attended school because it was court ordered. An alternative to community service was the Jacksonville Marine Institute, which is an educational program where at-risk males and females reside and redirect their lives. Had he accepted this option, he wouldn't have been in school or at the cookout on the fateful day that changed his life.

Thornton was dealing with the loss of his cousin, Pumpkin, with whom he was very close with. His cousin also sold drugs and had all the material things that came with the lifestyle. He was set up and murdered, and Thornton took his death really hard. He even recalls being upset because the perpetrator was never caught. Looking back, Thornton sees just how much the loss of his cousin affected him because he literally began to lose it.

He encourages any child who is dealing with the death of a close loved one to talk to someone about it and not keep those feelings bottled inside. On Tuesday May 15, 1990, Thornton and Marcel were involved in an altercation. Thornton and some friends had left school to grab a bite to eat and drink beer. While en route to class, Marcel threw a punch at Thornton and before he could retaliate the fight was broken up and they were both suspended from school. Thornton had no idea who Marcel was or why he hit him. The following weekend there was a party in Thornton's neighborhood, Richardson Heights. He was playing cards when he looked up and noticed that Marcel was there. Before the party began, he had been drinking and snorting cocaine. He developed this habit about four months prior to the shooting when an older guy he used to buy drugs from introduced him to the "rich man's high". This was portrayed on television in movies like *Scarface* and he knew other drug dealers that did it as well, so he gave it a shot. He admits in hindsight that using drugs was foolish.

Prom was the day before the cookout and Marcel attended. The next day he met up with Gary and some friends and planned to head over to the cookout. Before leaving, Gary said to Marcel, "I thought you couldn't go to the party because you didn't go home last night." Marcel responded with, "I'm already on punishment so I might as well ride." When Gary and Marcel arrived to the cookout, Marcel also noticed that the dude he fought was there.

Gary told him not to worry about it because he knew the other guys Thornton was with and didn't feel like they would let anything happen. Marcel was walking with Gary preparing to leave when shots were suddenly fired. It was dark and everyone began to panic and ran for cover themselves. While Marcel lay on the ground bleeding, Gary tried talking to him until the paramedics arrived. Fighting for his life and struggling to savor his last few breaths, Marcel uttered, "This junk hurt man." Gary told him to hold his breath, but Marcel did not say anything else. He was pronounced dead a few hours later. Marcel had just turned 18 years old and was scheduled to graduate on June 7, 1990. He had high hopes of enlisting in the military. On the following Monday, so it would seem like he wasn't guilty, Thornton decided to go to school. Coincidentally, a memorial was being held in honor of Marcel on the same day, but Thornton did not attend. He was arrested before the day was over...

After the shooting, I was traumatized, scared, I couldn't eat, really think and couldn't believe what happened. I felt bad, dejected and lost. I had a pager and people were calling nonstop. When I went home to face my mother I couldn't tell her what I did. She sat me down and asked did I do it. I didn't want to break her heart. She was at her limit. I just couldn't tell her. She was already crying and had been worrying for days. I told her I'd stay home and if the police came by again I would talk with them. No one called and no cops came by the house.

46

The following Monday I went to school, people were gossiping, I was noticed. People that knew me didn't believe it, some wondered what happened. I knew the cops would grab me at school. When I was arrested in a strange way I felt relief. I was emotionally drained.

A week prior to sentencing, Thornton had already agreed with his attorney, Jeff Morrow, to plead guilty to second degree murder in exchange for a life sentence with the possibility of parole after serving 25 years. This allowed him to avoid possibly being handed a death sentence. At sentencing, Assistant State Attorney Bateh stated, "It's the State Attorney's hope that this sentence will send a message to the juveniles of Jacksonville who all too frequently in the recent past have used violence to settle their disputes. We're hoping to send a message out that that type of behavior will not be tolerated."

During sentencing, the victim's father stated that he and his wife seek no revenge on Thornton Brunson because no decision made will bring their son back. He also stated he and his wife hope that when all time is served that something positive will emerge from his life. Thornton apologized to the family and after being handed down a life sentence that he'd already agreed to, he was taken to the holding cell. All he could do at this point was cry. The county jail sort of prepared him for prison life, as he was immediately faced with the task of defending himself:

Regardless of who you are or what you're dealing with, in the county you're going to get tested. By tested I mean prove whether or not you're going to stand up for yourself. I know this sounds silly with all of the serious crimes people are facing, but that's the primitive mindsets there. So in the county I had to fight.

Thornton was 17 when he was arrested for murder and 18 when he was sentenced to 25 to life. "The whole ordeal felt like dying. Remember how you felt at the most depressive moment in your life, your deepest dejection... Just to exist in a cage at all calls for some heavy psychic readjustment," he said. This cloud stayed over him for a while, but early into his sentence he attempted to redeem himself. He began reading a vast array of literature, including everything from religion, law, economics, history, psychology, and philosophy to Malcolm X, Nelson Mandela, Martin Luther King, Jr. and others who inspired him to become a better person. At the time, a scripture that he leaned heavily on was Psalms 51:16-17. *You do not delight in sacrifice, or I would bring it; you do not take pleasure in burnt offerings. The sacrifices of God are a broken spirit; a broken and contrite heart, O God, you will not despise.* Thornton soon found himself and the courage to change. As he began to evaluate his life and how he ended up in prison, he realized that he did not only cause suffering to his family, but also to the Findlays. Thornton says prison is rampant with a follow the crowd mentality, but he had to "keep it real" with himself and become his own person:

48

This hell is no game. When you're alone at night in the cell, you feel pain, sadness and remorse. This is the closest to being dead you could experience in this life. I can't reach beyond these gates (at least physically) to help my mother when she is ill, enjoy the warm intimacy of a woman or watch the sunset over the ocean. I encourage, urge every young teen to try and realize this. Life is serious and you must be careful. One misstep can cause you years, years of regret and sorrow without relief. Faith, family and pure self-determination are what keep me sane in here, from becoming one of the lowlifes and being sucked into the abyss of ignorance. Being a thug, gangster, or big time drug dealer is an illusion. It leads to nowhere, that's why you still see them in the hood. Be better than them.

Thornton often participates in a mentoring program where he shares his story with younger inmates who have less time so that his story can help others. He understands that he committed a crime that requires a great deal of forgiveness. In every correspondence we've had, he expresses this and makes no excuses for what happened on that dreadful summer day in 1990. However, the boy that existed then no longer lives in him. "It happened when I was in a moment of weakness (young) and madness (immature)," he says. It has now been over twenty years since the incident occurred. Twenty years of regret, twenty years of pain, and twenty years of tears, as his mother cries every time she visits.

49

<u>Chapter 4</u>

#P42243

Tyler Beall

Daddy Died, Momma Tried

**"*It was dumb to even get started on drugs,
but being young and dumb went hand in hand for me.* "**

It was Tyler's Bunkie that I initially contacted to share his story for the book, but after a few letters he and I lost touch. I received notice from Tyler stating that he had seen my letter and wanted to offer advice to the youth in order to direct them on a better path than he chose. He wants the youth to know you are not the only one affected by your choices; your family is as well. Tyler's mom even said, "It's amazing what you can put up your nose... your job, your house, your kids..." After our meeting, Tyler thought it would be better to draft his own chapter, and he also offered his artistic abilities for the creation of the cover:

I'm really not sure how to begin; I have never been too good at opening up and sharing my thoughts, feelings and experiences. I suppose you can call this my testimony, from my childhood until now. The pain, struggles, hardships, grief and battles with drug abuse that I've experienced throughout my childhood are all here. As children we all have dreams to be the best we can be, but what happens when life circumstances and bad choices get in the way of our dreams? Read my testimony to find out.

My name is Tyler Beall. Growing up, most people would say I had a good, healthy childhood. I was raised by both parents in Ohio in the same household until age 8 and then my parents got divorced. I had loving parents that took pretty good care of me. It was my older sister Rachel, myself and my younger sister Shannon.

After my parents divorced my dad and older sister moved to Florida, where my father ended up remarrying to his second wife who already had two kids from a previous relationship. I guess as you get older toward your teens you start looking at life differently and want to start doing things on your own. It was like that for me. I was so eager to grow up quickly. I began to do everything I could to go in my own direction. It all started when I was ten. I moved to Florida to live with my dad in 2000. It was my dad, stepmom, her two children, and me and my older sister, Rachel. Shortly after the move I started hanging out with my sister and her friends that she went to school with. I wanted to hang out with older people and feel like I fit in, and eventually I was peer pressured into smoking weed. After smoking weed for a little while I began stealing stuff like skateboards, bikes, and money out of people's houses. It did not take long for me to start smoking cigarettes and drinking alcohol either. I did pretty well at hiding all this from my parents. My dad was always working so he could support two families, my stepmom was preoccupied with her kids and my mom hadn't moved to Florida yet. The only person who knew a little of what I was doing at the time was my sister, but she really didn't pay much attention because she was in high school doing her own thing. Around 2001 my mom and younger sister moved to Florida and I ended up moving with them.

Even though I had to share a room with my little sister it was convenient because the school I was going to was basically in my mom's backyard. I always did stuff to keep myself busy; like skateboarding, playing basketball, riding dirt bikes with my dad and hanging out at the beach with my friends and chilling. At the same time I was doing things I shouldn't have been doing. I would get wrote up at school all the time or get suspended for a couple days at a time and not tell my mom or dad to avoid trouble. Most of the time they found out anyway. When they didn't, I would act like I was going to school for the days I was suspended. I would hide food and cigarettes that I stole from my mom in my backpack and hide in the woods or just skateboard all day dodging the cops. Before I knew it I was skipping school to get high and when I did attend I was in ISSP. My life was slowly going downhill and I didn't even realize how messing up my education would affect my future. I continued to smoke marijuana and hang with the wrong crowd of people. It didn't take long for me to discover new drugs and start using them; from Xanax, Lortabs, Methadone, Ecstasy and Cocaine. My mother and father would always punish me when I'd get in trouble, but I always rebelled. Shortly after I turned 13 my life took a turn for the worse when my father passed away on December 23, 2003. He fell asleep at the wheel of his car and crashed into a telephone pole and was thrown out his windshield and died instantly. I remember it like it was yesterday.

I spent Christmas Eve and Christmas Day at the crash scene picking up parts that fell off my dad's car during the accident that I still have to this day. My dad's death really affected me in the long run than what I led on, and to make matters worse my stepmom detached herself from the entire family. By the time I was 14, my involvement with drugs, stealing and robbing increased dramatically and my attendance at school naturally decreased. I was routinely skipping school, stealing, fighting and doing drugs which at the time seemed to be more important to me than doing the right thing. I struggled to do right once I started using drugs. I just stopped caring. I didn't care what anyone really thought of me. I also developed an attitude of indifference towards the world. This attitude eventually led me to more frequent and excessive drug use. Around the age of 14, I began snorting cocaine, drinking abnormal amounts of alcohol, smoking and doing pills on a regular basis. I began selling drugs to support my habits. I was depressed, stressed and full of anger and heartache. I couldn't find anything to take away the pain, so I did the only thing I thought I had to do. I became hard and hid my feelings and got high because I thought that was the answer to forgetting my problems. My mother did not suspect any of this, she knew I smoked cigarettes and thought I smoked marijuana occasionally but never said or did much about it. I guess with her working and me not home much my mom didn't see anything unusual. She had her own issues as a single mom.

I became blind to the destructive patterns that were shaping my life. The relationship between my mother and I changed in a lot of ways after my father's death. I want to say it seemed more like a friendship than a mother and son type relationship. I could then and still can go to my mom and tell her anything, but at that age I really didn't understand that. So I continued to lie and hide things from her. I can say my mom is the one person who has never given up on me, and has always been by my side no matter what. She has never really been financially stable, but as far as supporting me physically and emotionally she has been there. Over the years one lesson I have learned is to always listen; my biggest problem was not listening. Growing up my mom would always tell me, "Son just listen." I think when you are that age it is very difficult to learn from other people's wisdom. Sometimes it's better we learn the hard way. Sometimes if you're anything like me consequences are necessary. I had both my grandparents on my father's side pass, followed by my grandfather on my mother's side not too much later, along with two friends who I knew pretty well that died of drug overdoses. Death in my life and family seemed a frequent thing during my teenage years. I became good at stuffing the pain and anger that I had into a deep, cold place inside. I became good at hiding the pain; it was easier than dealing with it.

So it built up inside that dark place for years. My only reprieve was a pathological love and trust relationship with drugs and alcohol.

After dropping out of school in the seventh grade at the age of 16 I continued down the path of destruction. I got into a habit of drinking large quantities of alcohol. I wound up getting alcohol poisoning quite a few times, but there were other times I had to be rushed to the hospital, once by an ambulance and the other by life flight. The first time I was so drunk I blacked out and got into an argument with my older sister's boyfriend on the way back from a motocross show and said a lot of horrible things about him and his family, which caused us to square off to fight each other. Right before we were going to fight my sister jumped into the middle to break us up and I started yelling and arguing with her. I tried to push her into the highway with ongoing traffic (which I do not remember). My sister ended up pushing me, split my nose and knocked my back tooth out. After this I ran into a ditch and passed out. Next thing I remember I woke up in my mother's living room puking all over the place, then waking up in the hospital with needles in my arm and my mom standing over me in tears. Not long after, in the same year, I almost drank myself to death again. I was hanging out with some friends where I started drinking whiskey at nine in the morning. I ended up falling all over the place and puking all over my homeboy's backseat. My homeboy grabbed a hose to wash me off and sober me up, but it didn't work. I blacked out. My buddies got scared and dropped me off in my front yard, unconscious. I only recall waking up in a hospital bed again. I was tased by the police and was told I became physically violent and had to be restrained.

57

But of course I was blacked out so I couldn't remember. When I woke up I saw my mother in tears for the second time while I lay in a hospital bed. For a short while, I blamed my mom for what happened to me. Sometimes it's hard to realize the truth. Truth be told, if my mother hadn't panicked and called the police that day, I probably would've died. In hindsight I'm really glad she did. Getting tased by the police is the best thing that ever happened to me. You would think after everything that happened I would change and start straightening up. Shortly before all this I was caught stealing a weed eater and was put on six months' probation. I later caught another theft charge on top of constant VOP's (violation of probation) for failing UA's (urine analysis). When I was caught I was sentenced to a juvenile program. I was 17 by this time. For my violations I would be punished by getting sentenced anywhere from five to 15 days in DJJ (Department of Juvenile Justice). I was hard headed and still wanted to do things the hard way. I somehow managed to obtain my G.E.D. while in the program. Otherwise, nothing else changed. I did everything necessary to get home but nothing changed internally. My motto was "fake it to make it" while I was incarcerated.

Upon my release 173 days later in May of 2008, I wasn't much different than what I was when I first went in. I went right back to drinking, popping pills, smoking, selling drugs and not coming home making my mom worry because she had no clue where I was.

It's like I never stopped. I was on a type of probation called post commitment to ensure that my transition in society went smoothly—well, it didn't. I was working legit jobs, like McDonald's, lawn care service, and then eventually got a good job traveling building screened in enclosures over outdoor pools. Trying to make work full-time and partying at the same time did not work out, so I couldn't keep a job for long. I met a girl named Samantha, we got together in 2005, and around that time I was released from my program. We were going through some problems in our relationship with cheating etc., and she herself was getting ready to enter a juvenile program so we split up. Being in a long-term relationship at a young age causes a lot of immature emotional stress, so that was another excuse I used to get high and not care. I met other girls who were using harder drugs, shooting up, smoking crack, and even lowering themselves to prostitution as teenagers. By this point, I was living with reckless abandon and consumed by drugs, money, sex, and obtaining the three by any means necessary. Not long after being released, about six months, I was arrested again and placed in a consecutive program for another six to nine months. Right before I was locked up again, I went on a careless and destructive tear. I lost my mind and began using heavily. Shortly before I went to court, like a month prior, my friend Big John, who I called my brother because of how close we were, passed away right before his twenty first birthday. It's hard to even bring myself back to the place I was when I heard what happened to John.

I have never felt so much pain in my life. With my dad gone and now someone I looked at like a brother, it caused pain that is with me to this day. That pain has become a part of who I am. John was crossing the highway drunk on foot and got hit head on by a car that had not seen him, the impact was so severe it threw him about a hundred feet and snapped his neck and killed him instantly. After hearing what happened, it was hard for me to cope, because not even three days prior we were hanging out. Then, the night he died, he called me and told me he was fighting with his girlfriend and it was too late to go to his mom's house and he needed somewhere to go. I told him to let me take a shower, talk with my mom and I'll call back... I never did call back. I feel guilty and still hold on to that guilt (it's crazy how one word can change your life). After John died, my drug addiction fell to depths I'd never imagined possible. I would rob, steal, manipulate, and even resort to violence in order to obtain my drugs, by any means necessary. I'd officially hit rock bottom. I went to my second program in December of 2008 when a bed finally opened. Unbeknownst to me, an old robbery case I committed while waiting to go to my program was still being investigated. Through the victim and my co-defendant who was with me during the robbery, the detectives received enough evidence to put a warrant out for my arrest. When I found this out three months into the program I was really discouraged, because believe it or not I finally started to open my eyes this time and realize where my life was headed if I did not straighten up.

I was realizing how my actions were affecting my family and not just myself. In the program I was taking online college courses to obtain my Associate's degree and received a Food Handlers and Carpenter's Certificate.

Upon my release in June of 2009 I knew I had a warrant out for my arrest, so three days later I called the warrant division and turned myself in. I spent 23 days in the county jail on a $50,000 bond until it was lowered to $2500 with PTR (pre-trial release). My uncle in Ohio bonded me out and it was my mother who made all this happen. The whole time I was in jail she was on the phone with attorneys trying to get me out. After bonding out I was on pre-trial release which meant I had to check into a probation office once a week to make sure I didn't leave the state and randomly be drug tested.

Less than a week of being out on bond I started hanging around old friends who influenced me to do drugs. It did not take long for me to start smoking, drinking, doing pills, not showing up at home to selling drugs and even doing cocaine again. It seemed no matter how hard I tried to do right and want to get my life under control, I was constantly getting sucked back into my old ways and falling into the pit of disaster. It truly does hurt to know the unnecessary stress and worrying I put my mom and my family through.

I have always had good intentions but couldn't keep my act together long enough to follow through. It was exactly 60 days in September of 2009 when I failed another drug test.

Samantha and I worked our problems out and got back together. She too had just been released from her program two months prior. While I was incarcerated I found out she was pregnant. My mom didn't want to speak to me because of the fact I kept promising her I was going to do the right thing and stay out of trouble and I continued to go to jail again and again. When I finally was able to get in contact with my mother she let me know she's not always going to have my back if I continue to mess up. I told her about Samantha being pregnant and she definitely wasn't happy, neither was Samantha's mom at first, and she was very upset about the situations I kept putting myself in. She thought I wasn't ready to be a father emotionally or financially. I spent my nineteenth birthday in jail with no bond, family highly upset with me, and a girlfriend who was pregnant and needed me by her side, and there was no way I could do anything about it. It was very difficult dealing with the situation at first—being incarcerated while Samantha was pregnant and letting my family down. Eventually we all came to terms with the situation and began to deal with it. We found out our baby had died while still inside her. It was difficult not being there for her or anyone else. I was sentenced to one year in the county jail followed by three years of probation.

Although my intentions were good I became powerless again when I was released in May of 2010. I relapsed the same night I was released. I promised my mom I would be home for Christmas that year because the last Christmas I was home for was in 2006, that's including her birthday, my little sister's birthday, Easter, Valentine's Day, Thanksgiving and any little holiday in between. It was dumb to even get started on drugs, but being young and dumb went hand in hand for me. This time it only took a couple of hours before I was popping pills and drinking. The same day I was released I spent time with my mom until about 8 p.m. that night. Afterwards I went and hung out with two home girls and a homeboy of mine to go play pool and drink some more. I promised my mom I would come home that night, but for the next four days I was drinking excessively and hadn't returned home. I almost went to jail for an open container and underage drinking the same night of the day I was released from jail after doing a year. I ended up attending a friend's wedding, which involved more drinking. All I wanted to do was go from girl to girl, drink to drink, party to party. I told so many women a bunch of lies so I could use their money, cars, place to sleep, meet their friends etc. It was like I developed tunnel vision and couldn't see or hear what anyone else was saying, I was only worried about me and what I wanted to do. I continued to not show up at home and put my mom back to stressing and worrying because I would never answer my cell phone.

So she didn't know if her only son was dead, alive, hurt or what. I was consuming massive quantities of alcohol, blacking out, taking pills daily and sadly to say robbing people for their drugs and money. All this happened within a two week period. Exactly 19 days later upon my release for robbery I was arrested for another robbery without a firearm or weapon and violated my probation I was already on for robbery. I attempted to set up a small time drug dealer and rob him of his money and drugs. About 15 minutes after the robbery I was arrested at a local gas station. My mother had a premonition earlier that night, but of course I didn't listen to her when she pleaded with me to come home before something terrible happened. I ignored what she said just to call her from jail to break her heart once again and tell her I won't be coming home for yet another Christmas. I was so drunk and high off pills when I was arrested. I didn't sober up for three days which doesn't sound like too long when you're facing 30 years. It took like a week for reality to hit me and actually realize how much trouble I got myself into this time. I was offered a five year prison sentence for this new charge and my violation of probation by the state. Instead I turned it down and plead straight to the judge hoping for drug rehab and more probation. That was not a good idea because the state requested I be sentenced to 15 years in prison. When I heard that it was like I couldn't breathe. My attorney had to pretty much beg the judge to give me the five years that was originally offered if not probation and rehab.

I ended up getting sentenced to six years in prison on each case ran concurrently with credit for time served. I stayed in jail for two weeks after being sentenced to six years until I was transferred to prison. Once I got here it was exactly how the movies projected it—tall fences, razor wire everywhere, crooked officers cursing you out, etc. All that is going through my head is how am I going to survive the next six years in a place like this? Once I went through intake, which was very humiliating, I had to line up butt naked with twenty other men in the cold, squat, cough and be treated like a dog by the male officers. Then I was on my way to the dormitory of cells I was going to be placed in. I didn't know what to expect. All of a sudden I didn't feel so big. I was placed in a youthful offender dorm a.k.a. the "git dorm" for my first week to be classified because I was under twenty one. Fights happened every day. Waking up each day I wondered if it would be the day I will have to fight or be jumped. Fortunately, for the week I was there I wasn't involved in any fights. After I was classified I was moved to my permanent dorm which was another youthful offender dorm. The only difference was everyone was 18 to twenty one and we were allowed to interact with the adults. This is when I got to see what prison was really like; everything was about gangs and where you're from, whites with whites, blacks with blacks, etc. In the dorm I was placed in the inmates had a thing called put down or paying rent. If you weren't in a gang you had to pay them weekly or monthly or get jumped until you paid.

I refused to pay, so some things were stolen out of my locker—I found out who it was, got in a fight with him, knocked him out and had four of his gang members rush me in a cell. Next thing I know, a buddy of mine tried to help me, three more gang members ran in so it was seven against two. I had a few lumps on my head, and a busted lip but worst of all I had to go to the hospital because somehow I dislocated my ring finger knuckle which caused my bone to come through the skin. I told the officers I slammed it in a cell door so I wouldn't get in trouble. Six months later, a month before my twenty first birthday, I was moved to an adult dorm and just when I thought it couldn't get any worse with the gangs and stealing, I was wrong.

There was more fighting and stealing going on, as well as a lot of homosexual activity. Everywhere in the dorm men were kissing, holding hands, and doing the unthinkable. When I first came to prison the guards told me not to get tattoos, share hygiene or anything else because prison is 85 percent HIV and AIDS positive. I ended up going to confinement twice in my first six months and that is by far some of the worst punishment.

I was locked down 24 hours, seven days a week except to take a shower in which you are handcuffed when doing so. The second time I went to confinement it was for 48 days. Now almost a year into prison I have been transferred to a faith based camp. There are educational classes and some trades that will benefit me upon my release.

So long as I stay preoccupied and to myself I have no problems and my days go by pretty fast. Just because it's called faith based doesn't mean there is no fighting or gang activity; it's just less of it. As of right now, I'm taking advantage of any classes I can to prepare myself to go back into society and be a changed man. It is a lot harder than what it sounds like. If you truly don't want to change inside you are not going to, and will eventually end up right back in prison where you started. I'm sharing the mistakes I made in my life to let you know you are not the only one out there having problems in your life even if they are worse than mine. The bottom line is I wasted too much time on nonsense. I will never be able to get back these six years of my life I'm spending in prison or the time I spent passed out at parties. It's not worth it. You only live once. Don't do something today that you will regret tomorrow because tomorrow is not guaranteed.

Chapter 5

#P43249

Samantha Sneed

Never Use Drugs

*"I can understand totally about feeling hopeless.
There are still some days that I feel there is no hope,
but I have to have faith in myself and my future
outside these fences."*

While walking to get her daily dose of pills, Samantha noticed a parked car running and no one was inside. She hopped in and drove straight to a drug dealer's house. Once inside she noticed he was asleep and the pills were beside him. Samantha stole all of the pills and within seconds he woke up and screamed, "Get the hell outta here!" Samantha ran with the pills in her pocket. She was so high that she drove the stolen car back to where she found it and the police awaited her. She was immediately arrested on December 29, 2010, without incident and sentenced to twenty four months in prison. Samantha is the youngest of three children. She has two older brothers, Jonathan and Chris. They both are drug addicts. Samantha's mother, Kathy, is the backbone of the family in all capacities. Her father is an integral part of her life and has always been there physically when not in prison himself. When he is drunk, as he usually is, he expresses affection by telling her he loves her, but can also become belligerent and aggressive when he is sober:

My dad has been a big part in my life, even though we don't talk except if he's yelling and screaming at me, cussing me out, or if he's drunk. That's the only time I hear I love you from my dad is when he's drunk...

Growing up Samantha loved the outdoors. She would build forts and hang out in them all day. She also enjoyed riding bikes, go-karts and four wheelers with her brothers.

In elementary school, Samantha was always in trouble for fighting or disciplined for her careless attitude. Things took a turn for the worse at age 10, when her dad and older brother Jonathan went to prison at the same time for about two years. With them gone, it was only her mom and brother Chris at home. They both worked and left her home alone often, so she started hanging with the older kids in the neighborhood. Samantha soon began to sneak out to smoke weed and drink alcohol. When her dad and brother, Jonathan, were released from prison she was 12. By age 13 she had already tried meth and cocaine, but claimed not to be addicted to them. Ever since Jonathan introduced her to pills she was on them from age 13 until her arrest at age twenty:

I can't remember the last time I was sober. I've tried everything except acid, shrooms & PCP. Everything I used I could put it down the next day, but pills. I tried them and haven't put them down...

At the eighth grade dance, Samantha smoked marijuana in the bathroom and was caught because another student told. She was taken outside and searched and weed was found. As a result, she was let off easy in teen court. In the tenth grade Samantha was involved in a fight with a girl over a boy and was placed on probation. At the age of 17 in 2007, she violated her probation for possession of a controlled substance (Xanax).

At this time, she began attending Emerald Coast Marine Institute, an alternative school that would conduct a random urinalysis, otherwise known as a UA. She passed each test with flying colors, but was still secretly abusing pills. Everyone thought she was clean. She would use someone else's urine or not use drugs 3-5 days before she thought she'd have to complete a UA. It was simply luck that did not get her caught in her wrath of self-destructive behavior. Once a UA was given she would immediately resort back to snorting pills because she knew it would be a while before another UA was given. Samantha refrained from smoking weed because it stayed in her system too long, so pills stuck as her drug of choice. In 2008, Samantha graduated from Emerald Coast and received her high school diploma. It was during this time that Samantha's friend overdosed on Oxycontin. She took six pills at one time and died in her sleep. This should have been a wake-up call for Samantha, but it was not. Even this did not scare her. She felt this could never happen to her because she did not take pills; she snorted them and she knew her limits.

Samantha even showed up high to the funeral and the burial site. In July of 2008, Samantha's addiction finally caught up with her and she failed a UA. From July 15, 2008, through April the following year, she resided at New Beginnings Youth Academy, a drug rehab/behavioral program which generally runs nine to 12 months. However, Samantha aged out of the program at 19 and was released.

Upon her release things started looking up and Samantha began working at Fort Walton Beach Development Center as a caregiver making $8.50 an hour. There, she worked with the mentally and physically handicapped, which was a lifelong goal. She always wanted to work helping others and follow in her mother's footsteps. Samantha went to work faithfully, but unbeknownst to everyone she was still abusing pills. During this time, Samantha found out she was eight weeks pregnant and quit using pills immediately, but still occasionally smoked marijuana. Two weeks later at 10 weeks gestation, she was told that the baby had no heartbeat and suffered a miscarriage. From this point on everything was on a downward spiral.

Samantha was angry at the loss of her baby and just stopped caring. She and the baby's father weren't getting along, and to top it off he had just been arrested a week after she found out she was pregnant. In addition to that, her father was also in jail again. To add to the mounting frustration, Samantha's sister-in-law found out she was pregnant and this made Samantha envious; she didn't understand why she had to lose her baby. She would lash out at her sister-in-law and wish bad things on her unborn nephew. Samantha was getting high daily to deal with her problems, but would still go to work and function. Her actions and her attitude about life were reckless and she didn't care about anyone or anything.

Placing blame on everyone but herself and using drugs was how Samantha chose to cope. In the latter part of 2009, Samantha was high on Xanax and ran into the back of a car at a red light, but the car was still able to function properly. Shortly after this incident, she quit her job and did nothing but heavily drink and use drugs. In March of 2010, the same car was totaled. She was so high after leaving a friend's house headed home that she ended up wedged under a parked 18 wheeler. After crashing, she left the scene of the accident and walked home leaving behind her car and personal belongings. Once she arrived home, she went to sleep and sobered up as if nothing happened, until the police called her about the wrecked car. Immediately prior to her arrest, Samantha was dancing to finance her drug habit. Since being incarcerated, Samantha learned that every day is a struggle living with other youthful offenders who are still not ready to change. Youthful offenders do not live amongst the general population and are not allowed to fraternize with adult inmates. They wear a yellow T-shirt and the standard department of corrections blue pants. Youthful offenders have to march everywhere they go and are screamed at daily by correctional officers. The program is structured like a boot camp. The girls are categorized by their behavior and also receive privileges based on their cooperation. Samantha battled her demons with drugs from age 12 until she was sent to prison, where she remained clean. She knows beyond the gates of Lowell Correctional Institute she will be faced with the temptations of the world.

Even though she is working hard to change, her environment at home will be the same. During a modality course in prison she was effectively counseled and participated in anger management. Since age 14, Samantha has been in a juvenile program, on probation or incarcerated. On September 29, 2012, I had the pleasure of meeting her as a free woman. When she walked out the gates of the prison, an officer told her she would be back:

"Glad you enjoyed your stay. It's a revolving door. We'll leave the light on for you."

With so many uncertainties, she knows one thing for sure: she does not want to use drugs again. Since her release, Samantha has been staying with a friend to avoid the temptations of being at home with her brothers. She is working a decent job and looking to further her education. Her words of advice to the youth are to be a leader, stay in school, and if there are no good influences around, find someone to talk to. Lastly, "Never use drugs."

Chapter 6

Anonymous Inmate

Speaking From Death Row

"Don't ever stop fighting for your students and never let your love be deterred. Some of them don't know how to fight for themselves or know what it is like to love or be loved. So they need you to stand in the gap for them until they are able to stand on their own."

The following anonymous inmate is currently living on Death Row where he awaits his fate. While he chose not to share his life story, he offers candid advice to Young America. He urges young people to stay in school and not choose the path that he knows all too well:

Some of you may know me, some of you may not. I am currently on Death Row at this time. I am writing this letter to express my thoughts and feelings with you on some things if I may. I hope that all of you will remain open-minded and not close your mind and ears to the things that I say. When we close our minds and ears, we shut down and refuse to allow ourselves to learn and grow and become a better person inside and out. I too once sat in the very seat that each of you sat in. I'm not that much older than any of y'all. I too as well have been in and through some of the very situations you have been in. I'm from the hood too. I've roamed the same streets and seen the same things that your eyes have seen. It's true; I am none of you and you are none of me; we are our own individuals, but we've walked many of the same paths. The day, date, month and year are totally different, but the streets have remained the same. They will never change until we the people, the individual, change them. As individuals we will never want to change it until we want to change ourselves. I open this question to all of you and ask you to seriously think about it. Who are you the individual?

Why are you that individual? Are you happy being the individual you are? And Why? While that is something I ask all of you to think about and answer for yourselves, let me say this to all of you. Having a thug mentality, dressing with certain types of clothes hanging all off of you, talking a certain way that's disrespectful to others and representing your neighborhood by the way you act and things you do don't make you tough and all grown up. Those things bring an individual negativity. Society looks down on them. They don't get no respect because they give no respect. They are stereotyped not because society did it to them, but they gave society the permission to do so by the things they do and the way they live their lives. I ask each of you this question: What do you want out of life? Tell me, do you want to be recognized by the number of people you have sex with? Or tell me, is it the amount of dope you sell? Maybe you want to be known by the type of car you drive. Please listen. Everything will eventually come to an end, especially what we call pleasure. It all fades away. Each of you is in a place, in a seat at this very moment that many will never ever have a chance to be in again. I know some of you are there in school by choice and some by force. But the people that will never be able to sit in the very seats that each of you are in have lost any freedom of choice they had, whether they want to be there or not. How? Because now they are locked up in prison somewhere and never have to make a choice about anything. Any hope that they had [is now] gone before their very eyes.

I know many of you know exactly what I'm talking about, because either you know someone personally or know someone who knows someone who is prison. Listen, I know it's hard for a person to change from what they live by because it's how we are raised and taught by others. Because it's hard doesn't mean they can't change. Anyone can change if they want to. I ask you another question: What is the most valuable thing to you? If it isn't yourself then there is a serious problem. That means you usually don't care about yourself, neither do you love yourself, which means you don't care about life choices either. When we truly learn to love and care about ourselves, then the choices we make and the way we live our lives truly matter to us. We value ourselves and other people. We first respect ourselves, then we respect other people as well. Life is never easy. It's a challenge every day, but it's from life's challenges that we have an opportunity to grow and truly become somebody that others will see, know, recognize and respect. We can get all the advice we want from family, friends, teachers, pastors, or whoever, but in the end the final decision is made by you the individual of what's important to you and what matters the most. Many people may look down on you because of the neighborhood you live in, the school you go to, the family you're from or the people you associate with. They will say you will never amount to anything. Let that be your challenge to prove them wrong. Let them know you are somebody and prove that you're not ignorant or dumb.

Take the opportunity that you have to get an education and elevate it to the next level. Step outside of the stereotypical box that they have put you in and create your own box, one that's filled with dignity, respect, intelligence, hopes, dreams, and unlimited expectation.

Chapter 7

#471779

Richard Hannans

Product of My Environment

"So I encourage you to listen now while you walk in blindness. I bring light to shine upon what's waiting if you fail to take caution and heed to the very warnings we all see before we meet the promising path of destruction and desolation."

Men in and out of the house, eating rice and butter for dinner and seeing people manufacture drugs or use drugs was not abnormal for Richard as a child. People were always in and out of the house visiting his mother, and she would send him outside so that she could also use drugs. By age eight, Richard affectionately known as Bump was being paid to turn the other cheek to what was happening around him. He was offered money by his mother's male friends to do chores and run errands. When his mom would do drugs she would send Bump outside to play. She spoiled him in her own way by giving him the things he wanted to compensate for the drug use. Bump was never mistreated or chastised and got away with a lot, as that was his mother's way of showing love. At times there was no food in the house and other times his mom would cook unbalanced meals that consisted of rice and toast. Bump didn't realize there was something wrong until he would spend the night at his Aunt Margaret's house. His aunt would cook for her children and sit at the table and eat dinner; she also spent time with them. He felt a sense of family and warmth that he didn't feel at home. He longed for this at home and would cry when it was time to leave. By age 12, Bump began to hang around older kids and started stealing. This became a habit because it was easy and he got away with it. In one incident, he and some friends broke into the Rite Aid Pharmacy and stole Duck Head shorts. Bump and all of his friends wore the new shorts to school. At age 13, a friend gave him weed to sell and this opened the door for bigger things. By age 14, Bump was selling crack and making two to three hundred dollars per week. He was beginning to get things that would take him forever to get through his mom.

Bump's street sense was well beyond his years because of all the things he'd been exposed to as a child. He had seen people cooking crack, bagging drugs, and although he never actually saw his mom use drugs, he knew when she was high. Bump loved his mom unconditionally, but was always angry inside and carried a grudge for her using drugs. He held his feelings inside and never talked about them until he agreed to share his story. His sister, Rachelle, moved out at age 16 and got an apartment so she wasn't exposed to it as much. By this time, Bump felt he had to sell drugs as a means for survival because there would be no money for bills or food. When he really started making money, he would notice drugs and money missing. Rather than her telling him this behavior was unacceptable, Bump's mother stole the drugs for her own use. During this time his mom was also dating a drug dealer who would have drugs in the house. This didn't help her addiction because the drugs were readily available. Bump once stole some cocaine from his stash and he hit his mom as a result because he thought she did it. Bump had to intervene and pull a gun to get him off of his mom. There were times when she would try to clean herself up, but changing herself and not her environment or the people she associated with led her back into addiction. At age 16, Bump and three friends decided to stage an armed robbery. He had a twenty four year old friend who worked for Wells Fargo and together they planned to rob one of the stops the money truck made a pick up at. They successfully robbed the truck at a Sonny's Bar-B-Q. Within minutes, the police were on their trail and a police chase ensued down Lane Avenue in Jacksonville, Florida.

The police were shooting at the car to slow it down and they were shooting back. Richard recalls the entire incident being surreal, like something you see in an Old Western movie. The car was filled with bullet holes and the back windows were completely shot out, yet Bump was not hit. He still doesn't know how he made it out alive. After the chase they got out of the car and ran into the woods while the police officers were still shooting at them. After about 45 minutes he was apprehended, beaten and taken to the juvenile detention center for two weeks where he stayed until he was certified and charged as an adult. At the time, he didn't realize just how much trouble he was in and thought as a child he wouldn't be punished harshly. He stayed at the county jail for 10 months, then pled guilty and was sentenced to 10 years in prison. Upon being sentenced, Bump was sent to Sumpter C.I., which at the time was labeled the gladiator camp. When Bump got off the bus he was told, "You either gonna fight or be killed." He got off the bus sticking to himself and he made it through the night. The next day on the rec yard, he witnessed someone being stabbed six times in the side. One time, someone was playing dominoes and was stabbed for no reason at all. There would be riots in the yard and the guards would lock the rec gate and let the inmates fight until backup came. Once backup arrived, they would shoot inmates with rubber pellets and spray tear gas to break up the chaos. After about two years of being incarcerated at Hamilton C.I. in Lake City, Florida, a riot broke out while inside the dorm and officers were engaged in fighting with inmates over a routine shakedown. A fellow inmate's personal items were being confiscated during the shakedown.

Richard decided to involve himself by helping his fellow inmate. An officer was pushed, so he was sent to close management at Columbia C.I. for inciting a riot. Prison was already hard, but being isolated for three and a half years was even harder. He was locked down twenty four hours a day, seven days a week, and only allowed to shower three days per week. Visitation and phone privileges were limited. He recalls this as being the worst time of his life and knows that it was God who got him through. There would be inmates harming themselves and attempting suicide just to be sent to a hospital and get reprieve from being alone in a cell. People would do crazy things just for some form of human contact. If an inmate gets in trouble while in close management confinement, the punishments are severe. One can be placed on property restriction where they are left in nothing but their underwear and the steel frame to lay on for three days with no mattress. Another form of punishment is when you are placed on a diet in which all of your food is blended into a ball called a "loft" and it is served cold. This treatment is not reserved for adults; it is handed down to juvenile inmates as well.

After three and half years of isolation, Bump was released back into general population where he served the remainder of his sentence. A lot had changed once Bump was set free. The son he had prior to incarceration who was only six months old was now 11 years old. During his incarceration, he had only seen him twice while his sister struggled to raise him, along with her three children. He stayed with family members while looking for work which is not an easy task for a convicted felon. He was turned away many times or never called back.

He signed up for classes at Tulsa Welding School and faithfully attended and completed the program. After graduating, he was able to find a job at the Ship Yard, but was laid off. After a few months of being laid off with no income, he set out to make quick money by selling drugs just to get the basic things he needed. It was never his intention to make a career out of it; it was simply his form of survival. He hated being a burden to his loved ones and at the time felt this was his only option. In the fall of 2010, Bump was arrested for cocaine possession and sales charges for serving an undercover officer. A few years prior, while riding with a friend, they were pulled over and he was arrested for possession and served county jail time. The drugs weren't his, but he took the blame because his friend was on probation. Because of his previous drug charge, he was labeled as a habitual offender this time and sentenced accordingly. The judge handed down a sentence of 15 years. Bump immediately began to shed tears, as well as his family who was in attendance. While incarcerated, Bump works diligently on appealing his case with the hopes of coming home sooner than the 15 years he was sentenced to. If his attempts are unsuccessful, he will be nearly 50 years old and will have served half of his life in prison. Richard constantly reflects on this unfortunate circumstance by offering meaningful advice:

One of the most serious decisions I've made in my life is the very same decision that framed my future. It was truly the worst decision I could have made as a youth. It was a decision, an independent choice to commit a crime I would soon regret for the rest of my life.

In the twinkle of an eye, as quick as I contemplated the power to drive the thought, was the same quickness that involuntarily stirred my future. Though the thought and choice to make the decision was truly my choice, my friends, homeboys and peers played an influential role in the process. Being young minded I didn't want to let my friends down. It didn't matter that it was faithless or true, what mattered was "being down". Within a moment, I found myself alone in the backseat of the police car being led to jail. All I could do was ponder on the 'what ifs'. What if I had said no? What if I just said, "I'm cool." I say this because I wouldn't want for another young man or woman to embrace the avoidable mistakes I made years ago. I was 16 years old when I went to jail, 17 when I went to prison. As an adult being forced to be a man at such an early age was difficult, challenging, and controversial; having to fight all the time, hearing the cries of those who were being raped and witnessing stabbings. Then later down the deep dark tunnel of my sentence being locked down for 39 months.

I tell you, youthful reader, being closed in a cell no bigger than a hallway was below the level of a beast. That's how it is in the chain gang, close management security level for the ones who rebelliously refused to respect the rules. Many nights, pillow burning with tears as rivers of waters flowed down my cheeks as many who could not endure tried to take their own lives.

The management of being in closed custody did not get easier for me. Not being able to interact with other inmates or talk to other people, even a dap or high five was greatly desired and missed. Not being able to see your loved ones let alone being able to call them was enough to teach any young person the appreciation of the small things in life. To give up the movies, the food, the proms, the graduation, succeeding in life for what I've now experienced was foolish and unwise of me.

Chapter 8

#J44302

Devonta Mayberry

My Brother's Keeper

*"At the end of the day all choices are on you.
Before you do anything understand what you're doing
and be ready to accept everything that comes with it."*

August 22, 2009, 6:05 a.m. forever changed my life as well as my family. If I had to describe how this has affected me as a parent, I think the words I would use are "immeasurable pain." Devonta is my baby of two sons; they are 10 years apart in age. Seeing Devonta plastered on every news station and portrayed as a monster took a lot out of me. I can remember sitting in my room screaming "That's not my baby, that's not who I raised!" Wow, just writing this brings tears. I just wanted the world to know that he was a good son, mannerable, smart and talented. He was raised in church and knew God, but it seemed as if no one cared...

Ever thought you could be charged for a murder you didn't commit? Neither did 17 year old Devonta, until he was riding to a party with four friends. His whole life changed in a matter of minutes. He and his friends were in a white Chevrolet Impala driving down Wilson Boulevard as the Jacksonville Sheriff's Office was in pursuit of a white vehicle occupied by black males who had just committed a robbery. In an attempt to apprehend these young men, the police drove up behind them and signaled for them to stop; however, they continued driving. Eventually, spikes were deployed to deflate the tires in order to stop the vehicle. Once the car was immobile, three of the young men got out of the car and started running. The officers proceeded to fire multiple shots. The shots that were fired killed Devonta's friend that he refers to as his brother, Tony.

Tony died on the asphalt in front of the car. For hours, Devonta sat at the crime scene with thoughts of losing a close friend, not prepared for what was to come. Everything happened too fast for him to fully understand, and since that tragic day in 2009 he has been incarcerated. He was arrested and booked for fleeing and eluding, robbery and felony murder. Felony murder occurs when someone dies in the commission of a felony, in this case, even when a participant in the crime did not pull the trigger. Although they didn't actually shoot Tony, all of the young men in the car that day were held accountable.

Sitting through the trial, I can't write in words how much that took out of me. I remember sitting in the courtroom and his life would constantly play in my mind, but I knew I had to be there for him to let him know I loved him unconditionally. Still today, I ask the Lord "How did we get to this place?" For almost two years, I was unable to watch the news because it just brought so much pain, and still today I'm unable to read the newspaper if there's anything in there relating to someone going to prison with long sentences (especially our young black males).

Devonta's mother and father divorced when he was 10 years old. They continued to co-parent after they separated and he would spend weekends with his father.

He recalls as if it was just yesterday working at his father's booth at the flea market. At the end of the day he expected to be paid for a day's work, but his father took all the money he made that day and gave him nothing. This angered him to the point of tears, and after telling his mother what happened he wasn't forced to spend the weekends with his father anymore. He felt that as a man his father was supposed to teach him how to be responsible, instead of taking from him after working all day. He hasn't spoken to or seen him since age 16.

Throughout childhood, attending school, church and playing sports were the primary activities of his life. He was a top baseball player on a traveling team. Even when his mother could no longer afford it, his coach paid because he saw something special in Devonta. In middle school, he played football, basketball and baseball and was even an Honor Roll student. The signs of trouble didn't begin to appear until eighth grade. Devonta began missing class, yet his grades and behavior at home remained the same. His mother had no idea he was missing school until his teacher, Ms. Miller, called home. Ms. Miller noticed that both he and his friend would be missing class at the same time, which raised her suspicion. After getting in trouble with his mom he straightened up and would go to class regularly. Attending school was only half the battle. It was when he was outside of school that trouble would find him.

94

While driving with no license at age 14, he encountered his first run-in with the law at a gas station. When the car door opened, smoke emerged and the police smelled marijuana. The car was searched and Devonta was taken to the juvenile detention center for twenty days until he was released to go home. In another incident the following year, he was pulled over again for going around an elderly couple in a double lane. He was cited as truant and charged for not wearing a seatbelt. One of the occupants of the vehicle was also a runaway. The front passenger was older and had a license, so he was able to drive the car home. The vehicle belonged to Devonta, but he wasn't supposed to drive it because he had no license, a privilege that was taken away before he ever rightfully earned it. When Devonta began high school at Ed White, the skipping slowed down and he was a starter on the junior varsity football team. This kept him occupied after school, but by tenth grade he found it hard again to maintain his grades and sports due to skipping. It was at this time that he decided to quit football. The administrators also noticed that he was showing up to school late and high every day. He would show up to school and pick up girls daily to take them back to his house. His grades were slipping and teachers also began to chastise him for poor attendance, though his actual behavior was never a problem. In fact, he had only been written up for tardies. There was one occurrence where Devonta and another young man exchanged words on the then popular site MySpace.

The school was informed of the Internet beef and advised Devonta that he needed to bring a parent back for a conference. Instead, he withdrew to an alternative program where he was supposed to finish high school. Devonta never returned to complete his education. In 2009, which would have been his junior year in high school, Devonta was enrolled in Drop Back In Academy, but was not attending. The following summer, his girlfriend gave birth to a baby girl. From the moment she was born, he was there, and would spend the night with his girlfriend to help her with the baby. Devonta was actually with his daughter on the night of the shooting, before it occurred. She was three months old and that was the last time he would see her outside of a prison visitation area.

It hurts to see my people leave out the door at visitation. It makes me feel like my life is on pause. I've limited myself on life; I can only do so much from in here.

August 22, 2009 is a day that Devonta's mom will never forget. She was awakened by the ringing of her phone and it was a detective with the Jacksonville Sheriff's Office advising her that they had arrested her son. Throughout the morning she had seen news reports of a police shooting, but no names had been released. She had no idea that her son was involved and would ultimately be charged with murder. Later that day, the news reports worsened.

His face was on every news station and it was revealed that he was indeed being charged with murder. This situation has made her realize that everyone who makes bad choices does not come from bad parenting or a broken home.

For years, I prayed and asked God why he would give me a son that he knew would make the choices my son has made, knowing how painful it would be for me. For years, there was no answer. Until one day, I was having lunch with a friend and I confided in her about the trial. As the conversation went on she said something and I knew it was God answering me after so many years. Her words gave me a whole new way of looking at our circumstances and gave me peace. Her words were, "Maybe God didn't place him in your life for you, maybe God placed you in their life for them, because he knew the choices they would make and they would need a strong mother to help get them through it." So today, although our situation has not changed, my outlook on the situation has. This has made me a stronger person in my Christian walk and my day to day life. It has made me less judgmental and made me realize that everybody that makes bad choices does not come from bad parenting and households. My compassion for people is at an all-time high. One thing I realized is that there is no assistance or counseling group to reach out to families in my situation. There are so many non-profits set up for the families of victims of a crime, but nothing for the families of those accused of committing crimes.

I knew the need was there because both families hurt. I prayed to God and asked him to help me help someone else who may be hurting like me and not let my pain be in vain. So I'm starting "Healing Hearts", a nonprofit organization that reaches out to families. This was my motivation to go back to college for my B.A. in Business Management to become the director of this God-given ministry.

Devonta's trial lasted four days. There were four defendants, four attorneys and six jurors whose lives their hands rested in. Each of the young men faced life in prison, with Devonta being the youngest. None of the witnesses could positively identify either of them as suspects in the robbery. The victim testified to knowing them from school and knew for sure that it was not them because he knew how they looked and knew their voices.

The jurors went into deliberation just after 5 p.m., and after three hours they were able to reach a verdict. They found each defendant guilty of attempted armed robbery and second degree felony murder. After four long days of trial, the course of their entire lives changed. Each young man was sentenced to 40 years in prison. Since being incarcerated, Devonta has lost his grandmother with whom he was very close with and still maintains a very close relationship with his mother. He gets to visit with his daughter in the confines of the prison, but she doesn't truly understand where he is or why he is there.

She only knows that Daddy cannot come home. He encourages every young person to fulfill their God given potential and make good choices; because once you're in prison it cannot be fulfilled. *"A lot of people I'm locked up with feel like being in prison is just the cards they were dealt. We deal ourselves these cards."*

Chapter 9

#09013018

Sophia Smith

Guilty by Association

Sophia, Her Girls, and Her Granddaughter
(on the day she was released from prison)

"I didn't know who I was. I was looking, searching...
and it was because I didn't know who I was."

In prison, there are so many things you begin to see in yourself that you look at and say wow I took so much for granted, and it took every year that I was there to find myself. I can't even begin to tell you how much I appreciate life now. How much God has changed me for me to see myself and say 'Girl, you're loved... regardless if anyone else comes in, you're loved by me', and it made a difference in my life because I was mad. I was mad at life. I was mad at the situation, how I was taken away from my daughter. Why? She was only two years old. Why couldn't He just give me that back? But He had a plan and a purpose at that time and I just didn't understand. He said OK I'm gonna put you away so that you can see yourself and know who you are and then you can go back and try to make a difference; not just in your life, but other people's lives too.

This visit was a little different than the others. I didn't have to clear security to see Sophie. I was able to pull into the driveway of her humble abode. She greeted me in the driveway with a smile that showed no signs of a woman who had spent nearly twenty years in prison. She was calm, poised and at peace. I began to ask questions as normal and when I asked her about regrets, things got emotional. She had only one regret, and that was not being able to raise her children. She reflected back on when she first got to prison and the idea of giving birth chained to a bed.

Sophie then moved on to talk about the daily phone calls that were made home to her children and the depressive suicidal thoughts that followed. We talked for hours about her evolution from girl to mother to woman. With each year imprisoned, she learned something new about herself that she wouldn't have ever learned in the free world. Throughout the book, I highlight the risk factors that generally lead people to prison, but Sophie attributes her sentence to God. Through incarceration she found Him and through finding Him she found herself. It took almost two decades for her to realize that all the while He was there. After being released she thought she would live happily ever after with her children and the past would be left behind. As soon as she got to Jacksonville, Florida, she was escorted to the Emerson Arms projects where she was initially arrested to visit family that still resided there. She couldn't believe it still looked the same as the day she left it. Then, once home with her daughters the relationship was not what she had hoped. They were not the babies she left behind and they had their own lives.

After only a few months Sophie decided to move to Central Florida where she wasn't reminded of the pain from the past. For the second time, she left her daughters behind, but it was for the best.

It was December 11, 1988, in the Emerson Arms apartments of Jacksonville, Florida, when a loud noise bombarded the door. The children were sprawled playing in the living room, and Sophia and her mother, Annie, were in the back of the apartment. "Police Police," screamed the agents as they immediately began to ravish through the small apartment. The Christmas tree was shining with gifts under it and the officers threatened to unwrap them in order to check for drugs. Sophia, her younger brother Robert and her mother, Annie, were handcuffed and arrested, but the police realized that Robert was not an alleged suspect and let him go. Sophia and Annie were unknowingly caught up in a huge drug bust that targeted the infamous "Miami Boys". The title was placed upon the drug dealers by a Jacksonville police team tracking the dealers who distributed crack cocaine initially in their hometown of Miami, which later migrated to Jacksonville, Florida. Once in Jacksonville, the Miami Boys dominated the Emerson Arms apartments. According to news reports, the drug ring was operated solely within the complex. To remain low-key, the dealers did not sell on the streets. There were about forty to fifty people on the payroll, including lookouts who carried pistols to actual drug runners. The leader of the Miami Boys, Causey Bryant, was said to not actually sell drugs. Instead, he managed and directed the entire operation from a distance. The police watched this operation for months to ensure that all involved were arrested so that the entire operation could be shut down.

On the night of the bust, 12 apartments were raided and forty one defendants were arrested. Guns, drugs and drug paraphernalia were all seized. It is estimated that Bryant, better known as "Silk", sold as much as five million dollars' worth of wholesale cocaine, which was in turn distributed through street level drug dealers.

They had flashy stuff, but it wasn't as big as what people made it to be. It wasn't as grand as it was and they put everything together.

After the arrests were made, the residents of Emerson Arms were somewhat relieved. They reportedly said the complex was quieter and safer after the Miami Boys were caught. Prior to the December 11, 1988, arrests there used to be armed lookouts who were paid to yell signals to notify the drug dealers when the police were on the prowl. There were often shootings in the complex leaving residents in fear to even walk outside their apartment. The Miami Boys had completely taken over their neighborhood by hiring young children as lookouts and paying older people to keep drugs in their apartments. Their absence after the bust made a difference for the good and the bad; while it was safer, the tenants were no longer being showered with gifts, and for almost 20 years, Sophia's family was still trying to figure out exactly what happened.

It was like being in the middle of something and not knowing about the transactions and how things were going.

Sophia and Annie had over 25 co-defendants and didn't know any of them, even though they were all affiliated with The Miami Boys. At age 18, Sophia was in love with the thought of being loved. She was dating a "Miami Boy" named Melvin who also sold drugs in Emerson Arms. During the months of dating Melvin, Sophia never imagined that this teenage love affair would cost her more than half her life. Not knowing who her real father was and losing the only father figure she ever had caused her to begin the search for love:

I was already broken when I went. Not knowing what love was, trying to find it in a man, and whether he liked me or not didn't matter. I didn't know that because nobody ever taught me. In my family, they just don't talk like that. They're not very open or ready to give you information about life. They just go on. I learned a lot of that in prison and it's sad. It's sad that it had to happen there.

She was looking for love in all the wrong places, and found that it was within herself some twenty years later.

Sophia referred to as "Sophie" is the oldest of six children; she has two brothers and three sisters. Sophie and her siblings are the products of three different fathers. It wasn't until she was 17 years old when her stepfather and mother separated that Sophie found out he was not her biological father. This devastated her; more than she could ever find a logical way to express.

Soon after, Sophie shut down and grew accustomed to keeping everything inside. She and Annie never discussed who her real father was or why she was never told the truth. This was the way they both dealt with things all the time—never expressing their feelings and silently making the decision to move forward—and Sophie was used to it.

I guess we didn't really miss a father because she was everything. Overall she was a great mother. I know my momma and she knows me.

It is important for children to express themselves and have a loving and caring adult to talk to when they need it most. Oftentimes, when they don't have this at home they seek it in other places and things. Sophie is a prime example.

When Sophie was in twelfth grade, there was a persistent young man in school who wanted to begin a relationship with her. Because he seemed very nice and acted as a respectful gentleman at all times, after about six months, Sophie gave in and finally agreed to a date. They went to the movies, and after the movie he drove her back home. While still in the car in front of her apartment building, the young man forcefully attempted to rape her. She was able to fight him off and jumped out of the car running and crying. Another guy who frequently hung in the Emerson Arms apartments witnessed her in tears and asked if she was okay. At the time, he was dating someone else she knew who lived in the complex.

107

Still, Sophie took a ride with him and he consoled her as she cried the entire time. A relationship soon flourished and a year later in 1987 her first baby girl, Dedrina, was born. Sophie and Dedrina spent many nights alone in the apartment. It was later revealed that Dedrina's father was cheating when another woman appeared at Annie's door and announced her pregnancy. He denied the baby, but Sophie later discovered the truth and they broke up.

Sophie quickly found comfort in Melvin, a neighborhood drug dealer who Annie nourished like a son. Melvin met Annie in Emerson Arms when she observed how skinny he was. She urged him to eat more, and frequently offered him meals when he would stop by. This was the norm with Annie; she always cared for her nieces and nephews and other kids in the apartments. Four of her sisters also resided in the projects with their children and families. One of them stayed there for 39 years and just recently moved in 2010. Two of them still remain there today.

Melvin would see Sophie and tell her that one day she would be his, but Sophie ignored his advances. During the year that Melvin and Sophie dated, the relationship only consisted of him visiting her at her mother's apartment and one trip to a hotel. He once took her to his house after dark because he didn't want her to know where he lived. The couple never went on dates or anything of the sort, but a few months into the relationship, Melvin became abusive.

In one incident, Melvin thought Sophie was pregnant so he pushed her legs all the way up to her head and held them there. Annie heard the commotion and entered the room. "Leave her alone! We took care of one baby and we'll take care of this one too," she said. Melvin left quietly because he respected Momma Annie. After this incident, Sophie would sneak out to see him because she didn't want her mom to know she was continuing the relationship. He continued to beat on her and treat her any kind of way, and she accepted it. Sophie felt like this treatment was deserved and she didn't feel worthy of being treated any better. Melvin would do things like hide her purse so she couldn't go anywhere. The most severe incident occurred when he asked Sophie to take a walk behind the apartments. They began to argue as he pointed a gun to her head and threatened to kill her. Sophie ran home and he got in the car and left. Her life was totally consumed with being in an abusive relationship with Melvin, both physically and verbally.

I didn't make the choice to just go to prison. At 20, I didn't know nothing. I was blind. I just went by what my emotions wanted me to do.

On December 11, 1988, Sophie's world came crashing down when the feds barged in to apartment number 272. They were taken downtown to what Sophie recalls looked like a warehouse, where there were about 50 others being questioned.

Annie and Sophie didn't recognize any of the other people being questioned, and waited for what felt like an eternity. After about 15 others were questioned, it was Sophie's turn. While waiting, Annie assured Sophie that everything would be okay. During questioning, Annie and Sophie did not snitch on Melvin or his crew. When Sophie sat down, the detective showed her a picture of Dedrina and said, "You won't see her until she graduates high school." She replied with, "I don't have anything to say." Sophie could not provide them with any specific details other than the fact that she was aware Melvin sold drugs. She was transported to the Nassau County Jail with her mom where they stayed for about three months until they were moved to the P-Farm, the adult correctional institution located in Jacksonville, Florida.

I can't remember how many years I spent in each prison because I don't remember the dates. I just remember scenes. It's sad but it's good too because I don't think about it.

Both Sophie and Annie were charged with conspiracy to distribute crack cocaine. Neither of them ever sold or participated in drug use, and they were not fully aware of the inner workings of the infamous drug ring that the media portrayed; they were just guilty by association based on misinterpreted dealings. When Melvin would call Sophie, Annie would tell Melvin she was cooking and invite him over for a plate.

During court hearings, the feds misconstrued this as her cooking crack cocaine, which wasn't the case. While awaiting trial, Annie noticed Sophie was gaining weight and was concerned that she might be pregnant. Sophie went to the jail's clinic and it was confirmed that she was in fact expecting baby number two. The only time she would see Melvin was at court appearances and he would constantly yell, "I love you! It's gonna be alright," from the holding cell. Sophie believed this because she was still in love with him. Melvin was not initially arrested with everyone else, but turned himself in when he thought that it could possibly set Annie and Sophie free.

God is in control of everything, regardless of what I think and I forgave him. I'm not telling you I don't remember. I didn't forget any of it, but I just let it go. I really thought I was in love with him. I didn't know nothing else. My emotions were so broken up and I didn't know who to turn to, thinking if I didn't have him, I needed somebody. I felt like that was the only way for people to show you that they love you and it was the wrong answer.

Sophie recalls Annie losing about 50 pounds the first six months because she was worried about her other five children who ranged from ages 15 to 8 months old. At sentencing, Sophie waddled in front of the judge eight months pregnant; however, he did not show much sympathy when handing down a sentence of 360 months.

Sophie didn't cry or show any emotion. She simply recalls feeling numb after hearing her fate, and asking the judge if she could serve her mother's time for her. The judge advised her he could not allow that. Once back at the jail Sophie and Annie didn't discuss what had just happened. The dynamic of their relationship was still unwavering, as they continued to hold things inside and chose not to deal with issues verbally.

A few weeks after sentencing, Annie and Sophie were on a plane to Lexington, Kentucky, where they served about six years. Not long after arriving in Kentucky, Sophie gave birth to her second baby girl on August 23, 1989, and named her Melvina after her father. She was handcuffed to the hospital bed until the doctor told the officers she could not have a baby while constrained, so they uncuffed her. She stayed in the hospital for two days and was sent back to prison without her baby. On August 26, 1989, her aunt arrived to pick up Melvina and she took her to see Sophie one last time. She didn't see Melvina again until she was two years old. Sophie had the option of keeping Melvina in prison with her for a year to build a motherly bond, or allow her to stay with Melvin's family in Miami, Florida. She never had to explore these options because her aunt willingly accepted the responsibility of raising Melvina. She also did not want her girls to be separated. This was the hardest time for Sophie, giving birth to a baby and being stripped away from her at birth.

Sophie called to check on the girls usually two to three times a day, but the calls eventually dwindled because she didn't think they understood who she was or why she was calling. So she began looking forward rather than looking back, because it gave her suicidal thoughts. Her kids and seeing them one day was her only motivation.

For the first year, Melvin and Sophie corresponded in prison. In her mind they were still a couple and she still had hopes of going home to rekindle their relationship. He frequently asked her how she and Annie were doing and she sent him pictures of Melvina. Eventually, their relationship ended because Sophie started reflecting on how she actually ended up in prison. The family couldn't afford to visit often because they were so far away. Over the years, Sophie may have seen them a total of 10 times. They did however send pictures, write letters and talk on the phone on occasion. Sophie also sent videos home to the girls. To take her mind off of things, she began taking educational classes and painting.

I made a decision and I have to live with it. I just hate that I missed the in-between.

The next three to five years were spent in Danbury, Connecticut, where Annie and Sophie remained together. They never requested to be together, it just ended up that way and Sophie believes it was God's plan. "Prison is like hell with no fire," she said.

Without her mom there the time would have without a doubt been a lot harder to endure. During this time, she doesn't believe the family visited at all. Normally, towards the end of the inmate's sentence they are offered the option to move closer to home. With 20 years left, this was never a thought for Sophie and Annie. However, they were surprisingly transferred to Tallahassee, Florida, which is about two hours away from Jacksonville.

Once in Tallahassee, they began going to church services and practicing their faith. Sophie joined the choir and Annie received her high school diploma. They developed relationships with a lot of inmates who encouraged them to find Christ. Annie also learned to knit and crochet. It was also in Tallahassee that Sophie started exercising three times a day. Most days consisted of going to work, exercising, calling to check on the kids and going to church. Sophie did a lot of growing up in prison and although it took years, she learned how to love herself when she realized that God loved her no matter what.

The last years of their sentence were spent in Coleman, Florida. Sophie still sang in the choir and started traveling to churches, singing, and fellowshipping with other Christians she met. When the choir sang at churches, they weren't alienated or treated like inmates. They even ate afterwards and conversed with members before going back to the facility.

A fellow inmate filed a motion to reduce the sentence on Sophie's behalf in 2008 and it was denied. At that point, Sophie had accepted that she would spend the remaining years of her sentence in prison. This did not come as a shock to Sophie or disappoint her. However, in March of 2008, she and Annie received an order from the same judge that sentenced them, stating that their sentence would be corrected and no action was needed on their behalf. They didn't fully understand the legal terminology so they let someone else read it and realized that they would be going home. Sophie refused to get excited and filed the letter away. On April 28, 2008, both Sophie and Annie were released from prison after serving 19 years and four months together. When they walked out of the front door of the prison, some of the family members they left in apartment number 272 in Emerson Arms in 1988 were all standing there, including Sophie's brother Robert, her sister, her daughters, and the aunt who raised them. The detective was right; the girls had both graduated high school when she was released.

Sophie grew up in prison and decided to finally break the cycle of hiding and ignoring emotions. She and Annie began their communication breakthrough just before being released from prison and started talking about all the things that were left unsaid over the years. Today, Sophie proudly addresses her as her best friend.

We were always close, but it was always something that was not said, and today we're the best of friends.

Her relationship with her girls is slowly but surely improving. While residing under the same roof together for a few months, she realized they were no longer the babies she was taken away from. Unable to deal with the vacant memories of missed time, Sophie made the tough decision to move to Apopka, Florida. She hoped for a fresh start, away from the environment that frequently reminded her of her past. A Pastor she met while incarcerated offered her an in-law suite behind the home of one of his church members. She has maintained herself for the past four years, and travels to visit them once every month.

I didn't come out looking for grown girls that had already grew up on me. I came back looking for my two year old and my two day old child. I came back looking to give them something, but they were already grown up and I had to live. I had to find myself, even though I didn't really want to come here. It wasn't to hurt them. I believe that my making this decision did hurt, but it also helped me. I found out a lot about myself and I can say I'm ready to go home now and just be with my granddaughter because right now that's my focus. She's my focus. Right now she's my everything. I love children and I wish I could have raised mine, but I didn't. So now she's my second chance to give.

Sophie has no regrets and feels like the years spent in prison were necessary for her to find herself and build a relationship with God and Annie. Today, when she visits home she spends most of her time with her granddaughter, Sha'Niyaa, and her new grandson, Ja'Vant, who was conceived during the process of obtaining her story. Sophie believes that this is God's way of giving her a second chance to make up for the time and memories she missed in her own children's lives. She still hopes that they will someday forgive her for the pain she caused, and tries her best to secure a special place in their hearts.

When I first moved to Apopka, I cried every day for the first six months. I didn't want to be away from them, but I did it because I felt like I had to run. I felt like I should have stayed, but I just didn't know how.

I reached out to her oldest daughter, Dedrina, to request her thoughts on her mom's incarceration, and she decided to express her feelings in a poem:

When asked to open up
about my feelings
I didn't know what to say
Never even contemplated
what I truly felt
until today

Repressed anger,
not all from the years that we spent apart
It's the recent abandonment
that is hurting my heart
19 years
My mother and grandmother
were imprisoned

Well taken care of
but something inside me was always missing
I remember collect calls, letters,
and weekend visits

To me, after a while
it seemed like most of the family
was quick to forget it
I often kept my feelings inside
about the whole situation,
mainly because I didn't want to add
anymore guilt to the equation

Oddly enough I was never really ashamed
about my mom being in jail
Often felt misunderstood and alone,
but who could I tell?

No bond formed
because I never knew who she was
Sometimes I felt closer
when the bars separated us

Missing an integral part in my life
that we can't get back
Poor decisions and drugs
were the key factors in that
She was absent for most of my firsts in life
Never had the opportunity to tuck me in at night

No embarrassing talks about boys
or her just being around,
so I seemed to be normal,
but inside I was down

Suicidal thoughts
would often cross my mind
I would rather make her proud
so I never crossed that line

I have no problem forgiving
the mistakes from the past
It's how we are handling the present
that is killing us fast

Forced to be apart
by the Justice of the Peace
All those years apart never prepared us
for the release

I was the one that showed the most love
while she was away
My little sister, born in prison,
never had much to say
Never understood her cold shoulder
until it became my own

Never addressed the pain
always suppressed it
Now I'm grown

Funny thing is,
my little sister is showing more love
and understanding nowadays
while I'm harboring hurt
and feeling abandoned always
Because she left us again
after being away for so long
I thought we were a good reason
for her to come home

Moving out of town probably cost more
than we ever gained
Feeling like I wasn't good enough
so my actions and words are strained

It seems like there is too much pain
that we are all feeling,
and I don't know how to fix it
and start the healing

The relationship suffered
when I was two years old,
but got severed 19 years later
Maybe I will follow my little sister's lead
and let God take over
because His power is much greater

<u>Chapter 10</u>

#19661-018

David Goodman

The Hustler, The Rapper, The Man

"Drugs are alternates to happiness missed from those we love or long to love. They are the nexus of poverty and wealth to those that are inanimate of their surroundings."

Until age three, David Goodman lived in Waycross, Georgia, with his mother, father and three siblings. Being the youngest of four proved to be a gift and a curse. As a child, he would get away with things, and other times his mother was harder on him. His mother, Mary, was outspoken, aggressive and bossy while his father was mild and loving. The marriage proved to be tumultuous and they ended up getting a divorce. Early on David resented his father for this, but as he grew to know his mother's ways he learned to understand.

Once the family relocated to Jacksonville, Florida, they moved frequently and would often have to borrow electricity from neighbors through the use of extension cords when the power was disconnected. David was very smart academically and enjoyed school. However, other kids picked on him and called him "Dirty Dave" because of the clothes his mom would purchase from Pic N' Save. Being short, little and poor worked on his psyche.

When mom would go on gambling binges, sometimes she wouldn't return home for three days. I would steal lunch meat and flour from Big Star to keep us fed.

This fueled his fire and made him want to be better than everyone else. As a result, he used his talents in wrestling, football and basketball, but soon quit because no one showed interest by attending his games.

Mom was too busy gambling and my brothers and sisters were living their own lives.

Nearly 10 years later his mother remarried a man named Stan. He was a good guy and treated David fairly; however, he introduced his mother to crack cocaine. For this reason, he hated Stan and the way he treated him reflected his sentiments. He once caught them getting high together in their bedroom and he was so angry he began throwing things.

When I walked in on her and my stepfather smoking, I lost respect for everything living and my heart was broken.

After the drug use began, all of the things you love about a mother started to fade. The family outings came to a halt and she could no longer be trusted with money. Although the drugs affected him deeply, David thought after seeing his nephew sell them so easily he could sell them to pull himself and his mother out of the situation they were in. The crack epidemic was prevalent in just about every poor black neighborhood.

Crack turned dirty boys into kingpins, pretty girls into tricks, baby mommas into drug addicts. It came with a storm, and when it rained it poured. The people we knew as good neighbors turned into junkies.

Oftentimes, David tried to get his mother off of drugs. He bought her a house and also furnished it and even sent her to rehab. She would be okay for a while, but slowly drifted back into addiction. David desperately longed for her to change. Even with her addiction she gave excellent advice and guidance about life and supported his every endeavor, though many families were destroyed during this time as a result of crack cocaine.

She was an excellent parent, the best mother in the world. She made me the man I am today and I truly admire her for it...

The Hustler

At age 17, during his junior year, David worked at Krystal's, but was still selling drugs on the side. He saved his checks from Krystal's for college and kept the money in a safe at home. He had eighteen hundred dollars saved when his mom found the safe and stole all of it. After three days she returned home and would not even look him in the eye. This angered him so much that he moved in with his close friend, James, and his uncle and never turned back. With no money and his plan of going to college shattered, he decided to enlist in the military. Still hustling and going to school solely on self-determination, he successfully completed high school. After taking the MEPS test for the military and failing by testing positive for cocaine, he then graduated to the streets.

My mother was an addict so I had to force myself to finish school and once I did I thought that was it, so I graduated to the streets and got rich, but with that money I lost friends, family, associates and myself.

While trying to make a quick come up, he and some friends discovered a large amount of cocaine. He tried snorting it for the first time and liked it. This quickly became a habit as he snorted the party drug on occasion. He loved the power the streets gave him because people respected him.

To David, respect was more important than power or attention because if you weren't feared in the streets then people wouldn't pay you the money that was due to you. This power was an unknown entity to growing up in poverty that drew him in even deeper.

Those that didn't like me and used to talk about me ended up being subservient to me and I loved it.

In one incident at age 19, David was arrested in a sting operation. He served an undercover officer crack cocaine and ended up going to prison for 13 months. After being released, he immediately went back to what he knew best: the streets. Again, at age twenty two, David was at the mall with some friends when the police searched the car and found drugs and a firearm. He was the only one who ended up in prison after being charged with possession of a firearm by a convicted felon and was sentenced to 15 months. He wanted to end this vicious cycle and find a means to legally make money, so this time after being released, he bought a carwash, lawn service, game room and a seafood market, which was a lucrative business until trouble found him yet again in 1996. He was no longer selling drugs, legally making money, but still getting high with friends and associating with people who were still in the game.

You're either in or out. If you're having doubts it's time to stop and I didn't so here I am.

After his home was broken into, David and some friends were at the house getting high when an altercation ensued between two of them.

One of the men named Wayne began to act crazy and it annoyed David, so he stepped outside so that it wouldn't blow his high. After only a few seconds, he heard gunshots. The police were called and once they arrived they searched the house and found cocaine residue amongst other paraphernalia. This time around he was charged with managing and making available as an owner use of property used for manufacturing cocaine. David felt horribly that his friend was killed in his house by another friend of his. He went to the funeral and the family of the deceased thought he had a lot of nerve to be there, as they felt it was his fault or that he had something to do with it.

The only fun I got outta the streets was popularity, and with that attention and with that time!

The Rapper

When David completed his thirty month sentence, he opened the CTO Production Center and was headed for success, but he was still associated with criminals. What started small ended up being a successful local independent record label. He recorded two mixtapes: *Street Wars* and *The Balance of Life*, which can still be purchased online. Both sold a total of 20,000 copies. David was in contact with Sony and Universal Records at the time the last charges were brought against him, and was about to reach the pinnacle of his success.

He was on top of his game making music and making a way for other artists as well. There were six artists under his label and countless others in the industry who utilized the studio for recording purposes.

CTO also gave back to the community by offering free studio time to kids who made good grades, as well as donating school clothes to those in need. He was untouchable; or so he thought. On July 2004, while working in the studio occupied with twenty two people, the Feds came busting into CTO Productions. More than four pounds of cocaine and weapons were confiscated. David was arrested along with many others, and was advised that there was a confidential informant present at the time of the bust. He was so taken aback that he had to be rushed to the hospital. Those same people with whom he trusted and was around every day; one of them one was not loyal.

You know when you have people around chipping off the plate, majority taste that same venom and wish to eat off that plate alone, so you end up with more enemies than you could imagine.

There were twenty five co-defendants in operation "Chopper Stopper", of which David only knew one other person. He knew he hadn't done anything wrong so he was confident that he would be able to go home and beat the charges he faced. However, David was shocked when it was announced that he would be sentenced to 180 months in prison. It was hard accepting a sentence for a crime he was not knowingly involved in, yet still being associated with criminals alike. "Association is the biggest denigration," he says. Keeping it real was his biggest downfall; still hanging in the hood with too much money.

The Man

I'm 43 years old now and on my fourth experience with prison. It's a lonely bid. I have been gone eight years already. Once you're locked up you're on your own, but every now and then you'll cross somebody's mind and they will send you something to free their conscious.

Even your children grow up and out of touch after so long. They never stop loving you, but their lives begin and you become secondary. Since being incarcerated there have been four inmates to pass away in the same dorm. They each had less than two years remaining on their sentences. Then came life's biggest blow; his mother passed away in 2010 and he wasn't granted permission to even attend the funeral. In 2009, Ms. Goodman finally cleaned herself up only to pass away the following spring when she was hit by a moving train. As the train was stopped, she attempted to go under it to get around and it began to move, severing both of her legs. She died five days later. When David heard the news of the passing of his mother, he literally fell on his face. His son was also in a car accident and as a result paralyzed, but is now recovering. His wife has lost both her mother and grandmother and he could not be there physically to comfort her. All he could do was blame himself for leaving his family when they needed him the most.

I've been in too many gun fights because of a dollar and lost my way in life because of a quick money fix that was only an illusion to fill the gaps of a missing father.

With 13 biological children, prior to incarceration, David worked hard to reverse the cycle that contributes to the effects of being a fatherless child with his own offspring. All of them are grown with the exception of three, and he did not get a chance to instill principles in them; he just planted the seed. Currently, none of them have showed signs of following in his footsteps. When not incarcerated, he spent a wealth of time with them and taught them the importance of education. Even today he continues to maintain healthy relationships with them, as he believes it separates man from animal. He encourages the youth to always place education on a high pedestal. Everything else is simply irrelevant.

I understand the youth very well and I know the struggle they're going through because I am that struggle. Dealing in the streets with drugs, cocaine and weed, I've been around all kinds of people and seen all kinds of things. I thought money ran the world because it was foreign to me. I know their hearts and pain, I understand their thoughts and reasons for all things, but the one thing I don't understand is why it took me so long to catch on. Howbeit there is never a deadline on life. Most of our youth haven't seen outside of their neighborhood and the only world they know is right outside their front doors, so for any of us to reach them we have to know where that door is and what is behind it. Every house has a fiend, but who that fiend is affects a person differently.

After being released David plans to work while saving with his wife for a family business. He eventually plans to start a program to help the youth.

Spending time with his children and grandchildren and supporting them in their visions is very important to him.

Life is just beginning. I hope everyone learns from my mistakes so I'm not reinvented in them.

Epilogue

I can remember in the eighth grade writing an essay on the topic of disenfranchised voters. I didn't think it was fair then that after serving a sentence convicted felons still could not vote. As time progressed and I got older, my interest and passion for criminal law grew. I closely followed court cases that were publicized on the news in each stage, from conviction to sentencing. This became very real to me when I would watch the news and the people being sentenced were my age or had attended school with me. With every news segment or article I read came this nagging question: What can be done? I still don't have the answer, but I know I want to be a part of the solution.

Nearly two years ago I wrote my first letter to a young man who was 16 years old serving a life sentence. I could not myself grasp the idea of never being in the free world again as a result of a decision I had made when I was 15. I asked Jonathan, *"What gives you hope?"* He answered, *"Some days there is no hope."* From that moment forward I ended every correspondence with ***P.S. Never Give Up Hope***.

According to the National Center for Education Statistics, the national dropout rate in 2010 was 7.4%. In the state of Florida in 2010, the Florida NGA reported an 80% graduation rate. The other 20% simply fall into the oblivion of hopelessness and some end up in prison. In Florida prisons, the majority of the inmates are 93% male and 49.3% are African-American (www.dc.state.fl.us).

This can be attributed to the risk factors highlighted throughout the book. While the statistics show us the hard facts; the faces behind the numbers and their stories paint a bigger picture.

Over the course of the past year, I traveled the state of Florida visiting each subject in prison. It was very important to me from the beginning of this project to actually write each subject on a continual basis. It is not easy to open up to a perfect stranger about the absolute worst moment in your life that cost you everything, and sometimes it took months to gain a better understanding. With each letter I received more insight on why they ended up in prison. I then searched public records and news archives, spoke to their attorneys and even scheduled meetings with their family members. Putting these pieces of the puzzle together helped me further realize how life circumstances and the environment in which they were raised in aided in ushering them into prison.

Yes, it was a conscious decision on their part to commit a crime. However, the risk factors they lived with at home were very real—whether it's a single parent home, poverty, growing up in violent neighborhoods, the absence of a male figure, abuse, drugs or poor decision-making. Some may say these are excuses and that others have survived in more severe situations. My response to that assumption is there are exceptions, and the old cliché rings true that there are exceptions to every rule.

Then, there is the flip side to the story—those affected by the crimes committed and their loved ones. For there is a weeping mother behind every son or daughter in the casket with a life loss to senseless gun violence. There is a scared fragile woman who had a gun placed in her face asking for all she had leaving her paranoid to ever leave home alone again. They have to deal with the pain of the crimes as well, and could only wish to walk into a visitation room one day and greet their son or daughter with a hug.

It has been said that harsh sentencing deters crime, although there are no findings to support this. The grim reality is the harsh sentencing of the perpetrator won't ease the pain of the victims, and it won't influence young people in future generations to make better choices. After 10 or twenty years have passed, that young kid is now a man or woman raised by the system. They have matured and had countless hours of monotony to think of how they ended up in prison. By this time, it's too late; far too late to erase the past. The only hope left is an appeal, parole if eligible, or legislative changes. The one hope they all have in common is that the young boy or girl reading these pages learns from their mistakes so they don't have to make them.

It is my hope that this book makes you think of the consequences that follow the choices you make. I want you to see as you have read that you are not alone in the struggles of life. Don't allow your circumstances today force you into making choices that you will regret tomorrow.

To the young men and women already incarcerated: Yesterday does not determine tomorrow. You are told what to do, what to eat and what to wear, but you control your thoughts. Educate yourself and become a better version of who you already are. Read books and mentor another inmate so they too won't make the same mistakes. Don't let the time do you; you do the time. Encourage yourself and...

P.S. Never Give Up Hope

About the Author

Renata A. Hannans currently works as a Case Manager for Communities In Schools of Jacksonville and is tasked with the responsibilities of guiding at-risk high school students during the pivotal moments of their teenage years. Growing up in similar circumstances and surrounded by crime activity that often struck close to home, Renata was immediately drawn to the mission of assisting teenagers who struggle with the day to day challenges of peer pressure and environmental influences. She is extremely passionate about inspiring students to strive for the best, and vows to offer an infinite amount of support in the midst of equipping them with the necessary tools to succeed.

Renata's niche for criminal law was discovered at an early age, immediately stemming from her recollection of sitting in on her first trial as a public observer. Witnessing the legalities and strict rules of the justice system prompted an intense desire to offer beneficial help to young juveniles who face the long-term consequences of a life-altering decision. Fully aware of the racial and social disparities that currently exist in the legal structure, Renata strives to carefully lead young men and women who aspire to learn from their mistakes and become more than just a product of their environment. Renata humbly accepts her title as a role model, advisor, and friend to young adults who rely on her daily for a single ounce of encouragement, always reminding them to never give up hope.

CPSIA information can be obtained
at www.ICGtesting.com
Printed in the USA
FFOW04n2052050317
33021FF